SLOUGH
MAIDENHEAD & WINDSOR MEMORIES

Charlotte,

Please see pages 112 - 117 to keep the memories flowing!

Love from
The SLOUGH Legal Team
ICI Paints Akzo Nobel

28/8/13

SLOUGH, MAIDENHEAD & WINDSOR MEMORIES

The publishers would like to thank the following companies for their support in the production of this book

Baylis House Hotel

East Berkshire College

GEA Barr-Rosin

GF Lake

ICI Paints/AkzoNobel

Ragus Sugars

Retriever Sports

Slough Shopping Centre

WN Thomas & Sons Ltd

First published in Great Britain by True North Books Limited
England HX3 6AE
01422 344344

Copyright © True North Books Limited, 2009

All rights reserved. No part of this publication may be reproduced, stored in a retrieval system, or transmitted in any form, or by any means, electronic, mechanical, photocopy recording or otherwise without the prior permission in writing of the Copyright holders, nor be otherwise circulated in any form or binding or cover other than in which it is published and without a similar condition being imposed on the subsequent publisher.

ISBN 978 - 1906649074

Text, design and origination by True North Books
Printed and bound by The Amadeus Press

SLOUGH
MAIDENHEAD & WINDSOR
MEMORIES

SLOUGH, MAIDENHEAD & WINDSOR MEMORIES

CONTENTS

CHANGING THAMES: cruising down the river

PAGE 6

TAKING IT EASY: play time, with or without a ball

PAGE 16

TEARS OF JOY AND SADNESS: commemoration & celebration

PAGE 32

FAMILY HOME: royals in residence

PAGE 46

DARK DAYS: conflict and survival

PAGE 52

NOW THEN!: time for reflection

PAGE 58

ABOUT TOWN: unfinished business

PAGE 64

NEED AND TREAT: consuming therapy

PAGE 78

JOURNEY TIMES: means to an end

PAGE 86

MAKING A LIVING: people at work

PAGE 94

SLOUGH, MAIDENHEAD & WINDSOR MEMORIES

INTRODUCTION

For all of us, memories are the currency which we use to record the changes and progress in our everyday lives and to fix our place as individuals in the greater scheme of things. Whether our memories are joyful or sad they are the 'filling' which creates the sandwich of our life. Meandering through a pictorial cross-section of life in Windsor, Maidenhead and Slough over the last 100 years or so will inevitably remind us of the experience and success of our own lives, of our families and those whose influence and support has touched us to a greater or lesser degree. Whilst regret and loss play a vital part in our history, we hope this generic and random glimpse of the region will also trigger the smiles and laughter as you enjoy this journey with your family, friends and colleagues.

Many individuals, companies and organisations have developed and prospered in the area around Windsor, Maidenhead and Slough, in some cases spurred on by well-developed transport links as well as proximity to the capital with its resources and advantages.

We take pleasure in including in this book, histories of an outstanding selection of these companies and organisations, whose contribution to the development and sustainability of the region's economic achievements is a matter of record. With their co-operation and access to their respective archives, we have been able to tell their stories and hopefully trigger the memories of local people who have worked with and for them or been touched by their part in community life.

PROLOGUE

The establishment of a royal residence at Windsor during the reign of King Henry I is duly mentioned in the Domesday Book and, by the late 13th century Windsor had become a Royal Borough, enhancing the status of the town. The constant re-building of the castle over the next three hundred years brought in new people and new industries, thereby ensuring a positive future. After a dip in fortune in the 16th and 17th centuries, the renewed presence of royalty resident in the castle from the late 18th century brought back new life, although, until the Reformation, a steady stream of pilgrims had continued to make their way to Windsor. The castle is the largest inhabited castle in the world and over the last one hundred years has anchored a successful and well-developed tourist industry.

The building of a bridge across the River Thames at the end of the thirteenth century on to which traffic from the nearby Great West Road was diverted, served as a crucial early springboard for the development of Maidenhead, servicing the various needs of travellers journeying from the capital to the south-west. Later, the town's position on the route of the Great Western Railway ensured a continuous stream of visitors from the capital and was also instrumental in its development as a centre for river-based activities. Now part of the Royal Borough of Windsor and Maidenhead, the town provides opportunities in modern electronics industries and is part of the so-called 'silicon corridor' running to the west of the capital.

As with many other towns and cities, our towns evolved out of the natural topography of the area. The positioning of the three towns approximately twenty miles from the centre of London also had relevance in terms of the development of travel and communication networks along the Thames Valley on the western approaches to the capital, these accentuating their importance on or near the banks of the River Thames. The Great West Road, now long superceded by the M4 motorway, was a direct thoroughfare connecting London with Bath and Bristol in the south-west, long before the advent of the mainline rail network in the mid 1800s. In the early eighteenth century, Slough and Salt Hill were well used staging posts on the road from the capital, where horses were changed and the needs of passengers seen to. From a modern manufacturing site in the 1920s to a modern administrative centre in more recent times, Slough has thrived on its ability to adapt, both in terms of employment opportunities and its appetite for absorbing other cultures.

TEXT	DEREK GREENWOOD, STEVE AINSWORTH
PHOTOGRAPH COMPILATION	DEREK GREENWOOD
DESIGNER	SEAMUS MOLLOY
BUSINESS DEVELOPMENT EDITOR	PETER PREST

CHANGING THAMES
Cruising down the river

Our fascination with water is timeless. As a major element of the topography and geology of any area, a river dictates the positioning of settlements and a need to defend them against oppressors and provides a desire and a curiosity to cross to the other side. Whilst bridge building techniques are now more sophisticated, original crossing points, having been decided upon in early times, are often retained with later structures. Original demands for basic daily needs often meant that trading had to include a wider market and therefore, there was a need to cross, by boat or bridge, the flowing waters of the local river to satisfy the requirements of those 'on the other side'. In earlier times, water was a major source of power and a good reason to start a settlement next to a continuous and substantial flow of water. The River Thames has also provided local communities and visitors alike with copious leisure and pleasure opportunities and river activity is still an important part of the local economy.

Right: This appealing view, from the early 20th century, through an arch of Brunel's Maidenhead Bridge, shows a placid and relaxing scene of ladies indulging in a little light boating activity, together with their long skirts, of course, as well as their wide-brimmed sun hats – a typical River Thames scene at any time!

SLOUGH, MAIDENHEAD & WINDSOR MEMORIES

The proximity of our three towns to the River Thames has acted as a magnet on high days and holidays for groups of local people, large or small, for decades. Rain or shine, they have piled onto river steamers and floated up or down stream for a morning or an afternoon of fun and gentle relaxation. Philanthropic businessmen of the day would, once a year, offer this 'treat' to employees as recognition of their commitment to the company or organisation.

This picture of staff from the Curzon Laundry, pictured in 1914, have certainly dressed up for the day, hats and matching white dresses for the ladies, being 'de rigeur' at a time when normal daytime wear would have been dark woolly clothing, largely devoid of colour or any hint of brightness. Still tied up, but with steam on the rise and smiles of anticipation spreading from ear to ear, this group are ready for the 'off'.

SLOUGH, MAIDENHEAD & WINDSOR MEMORIES

Above: This picture of a cyclist, David Joel, riding along the ice-bound River Thames near Windsor Bridge, was taken on January 23, 1963. The river was frozen, from bank to bank, for a considerable distance at this time. By any standards, the winter of 1962/63 left its mark on the country: at the turn of the year, 20ft deep drifts of snow covered much of south west England. Fifteen inches of snow across the whole of southern England on December 27 had brought traffic and many other activities to a halt. As well as freezing over at Windsor, the River Thames experienced ice floes in the water around Tower Bridge and, over the following weeks, the night temperature across the country fell as low as -16 degrees centigrade. All in all, a tough winter for most, although, as we can see in this picture, unique and fun for some!

SLOUGH, MAIDENHEAD & WINDSOR MEMORIES

Above: A familiar view of the river taken, probably in the 1950s, of a gentleman pausing, perhaps for reflection, on the river bank. For those not into boating, the river provides ample opportunity to enjoy the more sedentary aspects of life. The closeness of water with its ebb and flow, its gentle ripple and splash and its unobtrusive role in the backdrop of life can be a soothing and relaxing antidote to the louder and more stressful impact of recent times.

Below: This view across the river, taken around 1957, clearly shows the extent of Windsor Castle, the monarch's largest residence. The castle and its various royal residents have contributed to the continuous development of the town, particularly over the last hundred years, as a major tourist destination. For those eager to taste its history and then escape the greater excesses of tourism, the river has long offered a conveniently nearby alternative.

Right: Another 'typical' scene of river life, this time an aerial view taken at Cookham in the 1960s.

SLOUGH, MAIDENHEAD & WINDSOR MEMORIES

An early and important event in the history of the River Thames was the signing of the Magna Carta by King John in 1215, on an island off Runnymede. Its place in the history of the country and the capital punctuated the next seven hundred years, attracting at the same time, natives and visitors to enjoy all its myriad and evolving activities over its 215 mile length.

SLOUGH, MAIDENHEAD & WINDSOR MEMORIES

In 1844, J.M.W. Turner painted Maidenhead Bridge which, in its own way, promoted the glory of the river. Turner's blurred and steamy image of a train speeding across the bridge epitomised perfectly the essence of rail travel to those still in doubt as to its effectiveness in competition with the tried and tested horse and carriage. In 1889, art in a different form continued the tradition of perfectly capturing the natural and emotional impact of the river. Jerome K. Jerome penned and published his eternal masterpiece, 'Three Men in a Boat', which, astonishingly, has remained in print ever since. Originally intended as a guide for visitors, it was quickly accepted as a simple and joyous appreciation of three men 'messing about in boats', full of timeless humour and hiding little gems of knowledge and oddity. Twenty years later, another literary classic, inspired, literally, by life on the river bank, floated to the surface in the shape of 'The Wind in the Willows', written by Kenneth Grahame and variously and evocatively illustrated in its early days by Ernest H. Shepard and Arthur Rackham. These two illustrators presented views of the river bank and its animals, so compelling and heart-warming, that the public have continued to demand their particular versions of the book for another 100 years! Perhaps the only other obvious parallel to this astonishing feat is the demand for volumes of Conan Doyle's 'Sherlock Holmes' stories, with the illustrations of Sidney Paget from the original weekly publication of the stories in 'The Strand Magazine'.

Looking back at the River Thames over the last 150 years, we see that in 1866 the Thames Conservancy was responsible for the management and maintenance of the river and they remained responsible for the upper part until 1974, when the Thames Conservancy became part of the National Rivers Authority which, in turn, was absorbed by the Environment Agency in 1996.

The River Thames has its source near Cirencester, in rural Gloucestershire, and eventually flows into the North Sea at Southend on Sea, in Essex, having bisected seven counties plus Greater London and having included two of our towns, Maidenhead and Windsor. It is the longest river in England, is tidal up to Teddington Lock and hosts freshwater and seawater wildlife.

SLOUGH, MAIDENHEAD & WINDSOR MEMORIES

Bottom left: This aerial view of Maidenhead shows the extent of flooding in 1963; not as devastating or long-lasting as the floods of 1947, but extremely damaging and painful for those living and working close to the river. The destructive and invasive power of water in flood has to be experienced to be believed. The 'capability' of flooding to disrupt and/or destroy people's need to communicate and travel is utterly devastating: life has to be, literally, put on hold.

Below: Taken sixteen years later, in 1979, this aerial view shows Maidenhead from the opposite direction, this time without the flooding.

SLOUGH, MAIDENHEAD & WINDSOR MEMORIES

Above and left: For hundreds of years, the serene and ghostly presence of the swan has visited the River Thames. Since the 12th century, all unmarked mute swans living on the River Thames have been owned by the monarch. Swan Upping is a ceremony carried out annually as a means of completing a census of the swans. Under a six hundred-year-old charter, the ownership of and responsibilities for the swans and the Upping ceremony has been shared by the monarch with the Vintners Company and the Dyers Company, two prominent City of London livery companies. During the ceremony, the swans are collected, marked and then released, but whilst they were originally a regular food source for the Royal Family, the swans are no longer eaten. Swans caught by the Queen's Swan Uppers, headed by the Swan Master, are left unmarked, those caught by the Vintners Uppers are ringed on both legs and the ones caught by the Dyers Uppers are ringed on one leg. This ceremony takes place annually during the third week in July and, as a fascinating and Royal link with the past, attracts regular watchers.

Right: Although taken in 1977, this view of the Thames at Marlow Bridge has the look and feel of a genteel Victorian painting, with the simple elegance and intricacy of the bridge ironwork in the background and, in the foreground, the graceful and historical familiarity of the river's indigenous swans.

SLOUGH, MAIDENHEAD & WINDSOR MEMORIES

TAKING IT EASY
Play time, with or without a ball

Games and sporting activity have changed radically over the last one hundred years, for both participants and spectators. Many sports have disappeared altogether and others remain by the skin of their teeth thanks to the undiminished enthusiasm of sporting fanatics. Money, commercial interests and media involvement have perhaps, in recent times, dictated a more cynical and detached view of major sports and control has passed from the enthusiast to those with a 'vested interest'. At the other end of the scale, as children, we now engage more in isolated and solitary electronic activity rather than in the simple street games of our parents and grandparents. Our 'chilling time', where we choose to take it easy and re-charge our batteries, has become more difficult to define and squeeze in between our various commitments in the hectic pace of life; for some families, even making time to sit down together round a dining table for an evening meal has become fraught with objections and myriad other more pressing commitments.

The electronic age has delivered progress and potential on a scale previously unimaginable; it has also ensured that conversation as we knew it, where we stood in front of each other and talked, listened, responded, debated, concluded and moved on, has become elusive, absent and unfamiliar to many. A hundred years ago, decisions were simpler: we didn't have the choice and variety of possibilities which we have today. There were many things we couldn't afford and so we did without, chasing the ideal, the perfect choice, was not even a possibility, never mind achievable. A more simplistic but honest approach to relaxation, individual physical fitness and personal enjoyment had its advantages!

SLOUGH, MAIDENHEAD & WINDSOR MEMORIES

We are sometimes obliged to remember that at the turn of the twentieth century, ladies wore ankle length dresses impeding their progress more than a little and yet they managed to do many of the things that they indulge in today. In the early 1900s, many people hardly saw an ankle from the cradle to the grave, never mind a knee and, shock horror, certainly never a thigh! But, guess what? – women still managed to have fun as we can see in this picture of the skating rink in Maidenhead. How ladies moved, from the waist downwards, was still a mystery to members of the opposite gender! Fashion at that time was more connected to prudery and comfort as opposed to trend and style. Into the 1920s, a more permissive slant on fashion developed, embracing colour, the appearance of ankles and new and lighter fabrics. By the 1930s, people had become even less prudish and were willing to be seen in their all-in-one bathing costumes, male and female, on the beach, even if they were still made of wool.

SLOUGH, MAIDENHEAD & WINDSOR MEMORIES

The 1908 Olympic Games held in London are accepted as the first Games of the IV Olympiad. Originally, Rome had been designated as the site for these Games. With an immense and violent eruption of Mount Vesuvius resulting in the devastation of Naples, money earmarked for the Rome Olympics was diverted to the rebuilding of Naples and the Olympic Games were reassigned to London.

The White City Stadium was built as the main arena for the games, with the running track around the internal perimeter of a larger diameter than usual with only three laps to a mile instead of four. The in-field contained, amazingly, the pool for swimming and diving events and gymnastics and wrestling also took place in this area.

SLOUGH, MAIDENHEAD & WINDSOR MEMORIES

Above: Previously, for some years, the marathon had been run to a distance of 25 miles, but here the distance was increased to 26 miles and 385 yards to accommodate a start line within the grounds of Windsor Castle in view of the castle's children's nursery. As a result, from 1924, this distance became the norm for the 'modern' marathon.

The event itself was not without controversy. The first runner to enter the stadium was the Italian runner Dorando Pietri, who staggered into the arena only to run the wrong way and collapse several times. Officials, holding him upright, effectively carried him to the finish line. The second man into the stadium, the American Johnny Hayes, was awarded first place and duly received his medal. However, Pietri was seen as not having been responsible for his disqualification and was, the next day, awarded a silver cup by Queen Alexandra for his courage and achievement.

These two photographs show the runners leaving the grounds of the castle and crossing the Toll Bridge in the town; at this stage nobody could have anticipated who would win the main prize!

SLOUGH, MAIDENHEAD & WINDSOR MEMORIES

Football at the turn of the 20th century was a very different game than it is today – although some lower league clubs might agree to differ! This photograph shows Maidenhead Football Club in 1911/12. Certainly in their infancy, football leagues were directed at the ordinary working man, whose support provided the main source of income. It is, however, interesting to note that some football clubs today are still playing on the same grounds on which they started out a hundred years ago. The appeal of football in the early 20th century was that it took place locally, with local lads and was a regularly available spectator sport: 'image rights' – what do you mean?

In Slough, the football club was founded in 1890, with the amalgamation of three existing clubs, Swift, Slough Albion and Young Men's Friendly Society. In 1936, Slough FC merged with Slough United for a time as a means of being able to play on a ground in their home town, having lost their original ground. However, after World War II, the two clubs separated with Slough FC becoming Slough Town FC. Slough Football Club triumphed in the Corinthian League in 1950/51, after which the team hopped up and down various leagues until 2007/08, when relegation loomed yet again. Thanks to the placing of Halifax Town into administration, Slough survived at the eleventh hour to fight another day.

20

SLOUGH, MAIDENHEAD & WINDSOR MEMORIES

Above and below: At the end of the 19th century, a well-known Victorian actress, Miss Kittie Carson, together with a group of close friends, founded Langley Actors Orphanage, in Croydon. It catered for the less fortunate children of actors who had died or fallen on hard times. After moving several times, the Orphanage set up in Slough in 1915, at a time when many actors had been sent to war. For the families of those who did not return, the Orphanage offered an alternative to the horrors of the workhouse. The Orphanage ran two homes, one for boys and one for girls, segregation being the order of the day. It developed a reputation for offering a real home as opposed to yet another institution for the orphans. Langley provided an amenable rural way of life for the children who became very much part of the local community. They took part in many sports activities such as cricket; here we see the cricket team in 1928 (left) and, preparations for sports day earlier in the same decade (below).

As befitting an organisation whose first president was the greatest actor of his day, Sir Henry Irving, plays were performed for local people. In 1934, Noel Coward became president, to be followed by Laurence Olivier. Later, the Orphanage moved to Chertsey and finally to Watford, until its closure in 1960. Its outstanding reputation throughout its history remained secure and a credit to its residents and the profession which supported it for almost seventy years.

SLOUGH, MAIDENHEAD & WINDSOR MEMORIES

Above: Now a suburb of Slough, Chalvey was once a village. At Chalvey School, in the 1920s, a school photograph was an integral part of the calendar. Having your picture taken was still not a regular occurrence for most children, hence many blank, cautious and enquiring faces. The idea of smiling whilst saying 'cheese' had obviously not yet been introduced and 'taking a good photo' came later, when photography had become a normal family hobby for most. What would these children have thought if they could have known that from the days of the Boer War in the later part of the nineteenth century to today, one hundred and sixty years later, we would move from a war photographer who pulled his cameras, dark room and associated chemicals around the battle field in a horse-drawn delivery cart to our individual wireless telephones with which we could take and save high quality colour images in a split second? The sound of boggling minds fills the air!

Right: The Boy Scout movement was publicly inaugurated by Lieutenant General Sir Robert Baden-Powell on January 24, 1908 and was followed in 1910 by the establishment of another organisation, the Girl Guides. A hero of the Boer War and intensively involved in the breaking of the Siege of Mafeking, Baden-Powell's military experiences were later translated into practical outdoor activities and crafts designed to encourage survival skills and group activities. His instruction book on 'military scouting' had provoked a great deal of interest amongst young boys. His new book, Scouting for Boys, also proved popular and underpinned the establishment of a movement that was to spread across the world and, today, remains an attractive and supportive distraction for young boys.

The disciplines of military service and training and their crucial role in conflicts had initiated the movement and the two world wars and lesser conflicts of the twentieth century and beyond, have undoubtedly enabled scouting to remain as an appropriate and over-arching organisation for developing practical and social skills.

This picture, taken at Langley in 1936, shows the local troop in their uniforms, designed to be informal enough to discourage association with their military equivalents but to be successful in erasing any evidence of social class or difference.

Top right and centre right: These photographs of Montem Open Air Swimming Pool, Slough, taken between 1930 and 1938, show a substantial outdoor public pool on a

SLOUGH, MAIDENHEAD & WINDSOR MEMORIES

scale we no longer see. In 1934, a small bathing pool was opened in addition to the larger pool. Whilst, until very recently, our climate is perceived to have changed relatively little in the last 100 years, we rarely have the optimism or need to create such fun opportunities outdoors. In the 1950's, the park-based outdoor pools, such as this, began their slow, sad decline into disrepair, never to be replaced, as other new and 'exciting' activities, largely indoors, replaced them. Cheap fun such as this, particularly for children, no longer enjoyed a place at the forefront of everybody's wish list – and this was long before the constraints of Health and Safety imposed their overbearing will on us all!

Right: Slough Secondary School was founded in 1912 and sited at William Street in the town centre. A year after this photograph was taken in 1935, the school was split into two single sex schools, the Slough Grammar School for Boys and the Slough High School for Girls and moved to two new premises at Lascelles Road in 1936 and Twinches Lane in 1939, respectively. The schools came back together again, on the Lascelles Road site, under the title of Upton Grammar School, in 1982. More recently, the school has reverted to the previous title of Slough Grammar School.

Sport has been a vital part of school life for as long as most of us can remember, encouraging team work, competitiveness, health and fitness. The photograph shows the Slough Secondary School Girls Tennis Team in 1935.

SLOUGH, MAIDENHEAD & WINDSOR MEMORIES

From the early 1920s, works outings at the expense of the employer became a fixture in the annual calendar of employees fortunate enough to have a boss who understood the need to nurture staff. Destinations varied, dependent on the organisation or company involved, as well as its location. A local horse racing track might be attractive to some, nearness to a seaside resort attractive to others. Public houses, frequented mainly by men, also organised day trips, usually to sporting events.

The closeness of the destination was an issue, particularly in the 1920s, largely because the vehicles involved were primitive charabancs, with rock hard, cart suspension and solid tyres. Comfort and speed of travel were not priorities! Aside from these 'disadvantages', the destination was largely irrelevant; who cared, as long as everybody was having fun and the boss was paying!

Charabancs were usually built as a separate detachable body with simple wooden benches and placed on a lorry chassis. During the week they often operated with a flat bed as a haulage carrier, converting at the weekend to a 'people carrier'. There lies the origin of hauliers cum coach companies; originally they used the one vehicle with detachable bodies as the need arose. Still quite a primitive form of motorised transport at this stage, the 'chara' enabled ordinary people to enjoy a taste of motoring in the 1920s; the sense of being able to travel further than they could on foot or by bicycle was an exciting proposition in the relatively car-less society of the period.

Here we see an outing from Flags Public House, in Chalvey, on its way to the races at nearby Goodwood. This 'chara' appears to be of the latest coachbuilt type, a little more sophisticated and signifying greater investment, by the mid-1930s, in the business of travel.

For most, a works outing which also embraced your 'other half', was a good idea, not least because it would be a rare trip out for both husband and wife – and it was free! In the early 1930s, a day out meant 'smart and casual', as we would call it now, but hats were still essential for most, with a school cap for the young lad on the left in this picture of the G. Case & Son outing. A kitty for a crate or two of beer would have been sorted out beforehand with maybe an additional crate contributed by the boss, for good

SLOUGH, MAIDENHEAD & WINDSOR MEMORIES

The annual outing for the employees of W.G. Bedford, electrical mechanical engineers in 1937 (below), appears to be a 'men only' venture, prompted, no doubt, by the genderised nature of certain practical vocations at that time. Pictured in William Street, Slough, before the 'off', almost everybody appears to be wearing a suit, including the man in the middle of the picture wearing plus-fours, a more sporting fashion of the day. Perhaps they're off to the races and feel a compunction towards smart rather than casual! At least they have a state-of-the-art coach for the day, looking not too different from similar vehicles still running in the late forties and early fifties. On the building behind we see the easily recognisable and iconic Hovis sign, still a familiar sight in good times and not so good times!

measure. Having shown their unswerving loyalty to 'Mr. Case and Son' for the rest of the year, this was the opportunity to let the hair down; to have a bit of fun with people you knew well, for wives to meet and make each other's acquaintance again and with the prospect, hopefully, of a spot of summer sun at the coast. Towards the end of the day, it would be fish and chips out of newspaper and a sing-song on the way home, a whip round for the driver in somebody's flat cap and an unrestrained and heartfelt 'For he's a jolly good fellow' for Mr. Case and Son. Home again, with the warmth and bonhomie of a good day had by all, looking forward to another year of graft, it would be a happy and contented 'goodnight all'!

The proximity of the River Thames provided excellent water-based opportunities for local workers, young and not so young. The Slough Trading Estate consisted of many considerate employers with a relatively philanthropic and supportive attitude to their local workers. A staff outing in the form of a day trip on the Thames was not uncommon for Trading Estate workers. It was pressure from these employers that had resulted in the establishment, in 1936, by the local council, of the Slough Social Centre.

SLOUGH, MAIDENHEAD & WINDSOR MEMORIES

Above: Having travelled from the Forest of Dean to America in the 1870s, James and William Horlick began manufacturing a patented malt drink for children, in Chicago in 1883. Seven years later it was introduced to this country and in 1906, James Horlick purchased a field from Eton College and built a malted drink factory in Stoke Poges Lane, Slough: production began two years later and over the century, its popularity spread across the globe. The factory quickly became one of Slough's most recognisable and iconic buildings with its integral tower set next to the railway line. The company's success enabled it, in 1961, to buy another well-known local company, Elliman and Sons Ltd. Horlicks was absorbed into the Beecham empire in 1961. Successive generations of many families in the Slough area will have been employed by or been indirectly connected to this notable and successful company.

Even by 1938, not everyone was convinced that the country would go to war, which meant that life in the 1930s

SLOUGH, MAIDENHEAD & WINDSOR MEMORIES

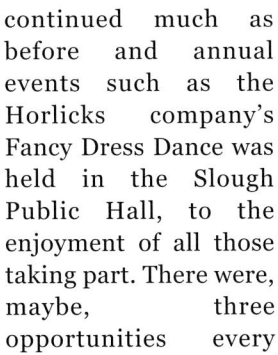

continued much as before and annual events such as the Horlicks company's Fancy Dress Dance was held in the Slough Public Hall, to the enjoyment of all those taking part. There were, maybe, three opportunities every year to get out that 'best frock'; once for a wedding, once for a family party and once for the 'works do'. It was the same frock every time, with maybe a changed accessory here, a new pair of shoes there, but nobody cared because it was the same for everybody in those days. A 'special night out' was special then, just because it was a treat and not every week. If you were married, it was an occasion to show off your wife or husband to your colleagues who you often spent more time with each week than you did with your other half! If you were single, there was always the chance that you might come across a previously invisible member of some obscure, hidden away department within the company, whose path you had never previously crossed. By the end of this 'special occasion', it was sometimes possible to speculate upon a conceivable change of circumstances; after all, working for the same company you would inevitably have something in common which could stuff the conversation satisfactorily for a couple of hours, giving you time perhaps to work in a more adventurous vocabulary with softer, warmer words, implying sensitivity, thoughtfulness and interest in such a way as to suggest the inevitability of a further meeting, somewhere a little more intimate and encouraging!

Left and above: Salt Hill Playing Fields were established in 1907, when the land was donated to the town by generous local businessman James Elliman. With great foresight, he also established a fund to pay for the upkeep of the Playing Fields. At the beginning of the 20th century, personal transport was almost non-existent and public transport limited in terms of its availability. Leisure was a word that had barely been invented, but people still needed space to play with a ball and play together. Many forward thinking councils understood the need to provide what later became known as POS's (public open spaces), giving their citizens the opportunity to enjoy the freedom of open spaces and to have a comfortable place to congregate. Eclipsing the two World Wars, this facility gave local people daytime respite from the confines of their homes and work places. Salt Hill, many years earlier, had been a notable staging post on the route from London to Bath. By the time this photograph was taken in 1940, there was not a horse or carriage in sight.

The Timbertown area of Slough, off Farnham Road, was an estate of single storey houses built in the early 1920s out of wood, providing reasonably comfortable and spacious accommodation although only destined for a short lifespan. The estate was demolished in the 1930s and the Herschel Grammar School built later on the site. Employers on The Slough Trading Estate, established in the mid-1920s, received complaints from their employees who lived in Timbertown that there were little or no leisure facilities available for them: these included Mr. Mars who rented a small factory on the estate in 1932 to manufacture his 'bar'. Through an initiative supported by these same employers, local politicians agreed to the building of the Slough Social Centre. The Centre opened in 1936, offering an impressive range of games and pastimes and space for wedding celebrations, exhibitions and much else. These facilities were well used and attracted a wide cross-section of the local population to an impressive building which cost a reasonable £45,000 to build.

In the picture, bottom right, taken in 1937, we see younger members of the Centre's cycling club about to set off from outside the Centre for some two-wheeled fun. We must remember that in the 1930s, cycling was a lot more appealing due to the lack of motorised traffic on the roads. Cars were generally exclusive to the upper classes and the working and middle classes made do with public transport and bicycles. It was an attractive form of exercise, particularly for young men, and cycling clubs could be found in every town and district. You might start off by seeing your pushbike as merely a means of getting to work each day, but, often, the opportunity to cycle for pleasure led you to a club. With support and encouragement from the early part of the century from the CTC, The Cyclists' Touring Club, founded in 1878 and currently enjoying a new popularity, many riders discovered the geographical and social pleasures of these machines. Membership of the CTC also brought you a fascinating and highly literate monthly magazine which was substantially instrumental in encouraging these 'pleasures'.

The Centre enjoyed a visit in 1937, as seen in the picture top left, from Queen Mary, widowed in the previous year on the death of King George V. Here she is greeted in Farnham Road by members of the Centre. A visit from any member of the Royal Family was seen as 'the seal of approval', adding to the kudos of the organisation. Despite the unhelpful poetic comments of John Betjeman, "Come, friendly bomb and fall on Slough, it isn't fit for humans now", the town continued along its innovative and successful furrow. A more recent and subtle joke at the town's expense in the shape of 'The Office' merely served to remind everyone else where Slough was! Most of the residents and workers of Slough smiled quietly, enjoying their success as the rest of the country 'took the Mick'!

The Centre, seen here in the late 1950s, bottom left, was renamed as Slough Community Centre in 1957 and a new building called The Centre replaced it when it was demolished in 1997. Several generations have enjoyed family and social activities at the Centre, in one form or another, learnt a range of skills and found new ways to relax.

Above: The Temple Golf Club was founded in 1909, the first club match being played in 1911. Long associated with the Oppenheimer family, Raymond Oppenheimer played for England on either side of World War II. He went on to captain the side on a number of occasions after the war and in 1951, he also captained the Walker Cup team. He was elected President of the club in 1956 and served in that capacity until he died in 1984. Many of the big names in golf at the time played at Temple Golf Club and the legendary Henry Cotton was appointed professional there in 1954. Two years earlier, in 1952 when this photograph was taken, Temple hosted a challenge match between the great comedian Bob Hope and Bing Crosby (America) against Donald Peers and Ted Ray (Great Britain), which was watched by huge crowds. Bob Hope who was a keen amateur golfer looks on anxiously after his tee shot.

Right: As the austerity and economic uncertainty that had filled people's lives began to ebb away at the end of the fifties, it was time to look forward and grab the opportunity stood next to you, provided of course, that it was happy to be grabbed! After the war, music became more important in people's lives, not least as an antidote to the relatively quiet times of spoken voice during hostilities. Pop music in all its new forms became a staple diet of every generation and everyone looked forward to the weekend dance at the Community Centre, often with a visiting band or group in attendance. Some will remember with affection, some with fear, those first encounters around the dance floor, the sizing up and potential of a prospective partner or competitor. The thrusting competitiveness of it all, those 'shall I/shan't I' moments, the shrinking or ballooning of personalities in the face of embarrassment or over-confidence, sometimes ending in tears of sadness and occasionally in tears of joy, or more often in an exchange of 'phone numbers with the hope that you could make it to the ringing instrument before your mum! The unrealistic

SLOUGH, MAIDENHEAD & WINDSOR MEMORIES

(always!) expectations and hopes of the girls set against the generally presumptuous and desperately immature boys could be witnessed at every dance night, typically photographed here at the end of the decade.

Above: The 'Army Game' was an extremely popular ITV comedy series of the late 1950s, documenting the lives of a group of peacetime soldiers, out to make easy money and generally 'taking the mick' out of their stereotypical sergeant-major, played by William Hartnell. As with its American contemporary, 'Bilko', the success of the programme derived from the relative closeness to the end of World War II and the change of environment for those soldiers who survived it. As today, performers on popular programmes such as this, became popular 'cult heroes' and in commercial demand across the country. In this photograph, taken in 1959, stars of the programme are seen helping a young 19-year-old customer, Marion Leater, try on a pair of boots at the opening of a new self-service clothing store in Slough. She looks happy as does Alfie Bass, at the front of the picture!

TEARS OF JOY AND SADNESS
Commemoration & celebration

We all, at one time or another, have the opportunity to take part in the commemoration and celebration of the lives and times of others. In remembering the lives of others, we celebrate their contribution to our own lives, however distant and formal. The opportunity to celebrate happy events with our friends, family and colleagues often adds to the joy of the occasion, be it a one-off or a regularly repeated event. Expression and sharing of our joy in celebration often provides the antidote to more sober and less happy occasions.

Royal events have presented, in the first half of the twentieth century in particular, the nation's excuse to party and decorate their homes and streets in the most patriotic way. At the turn of the century, the Union Jack was brought out for any and every celebration with no suggestion or accusation of xenophobia, although it has to be admitted that Great Britain did 'rule the waves and the world' at this point, with its Empire.

The eventual triumph in two major conflicts and the long-awaited return to peace for the nation gave added opportunities for unfettered celebration, albeit tainted, sometimes, with considerable personal sadness.

The intimate, long-standing connection of our towns with the Royal Family gave the Silver Jubilee celebrations in 1977 a very special impetus.

Below: After a quiet Christmas at her beloved Osborne House on the Isle of Wight in 1900, the ailing health of the monarch, Queen Victoria, quietly took her to another place, with her family gathered at her bedside, including her son, soon to be crowned King Edward VII, and her eldest grandson, the German Emperor William II. Victoria had reigned from the age of 18, in 1837, when as a slim young girl she began a quietly relentless rule and oversaw the global expansion of the British Empire. Victoria reigned for an almost inconceivable sixty three years, out-stripping her grandfather George III as the longest lived monarch by three days. It is, perhaps, no surprise that this period in history is referred to as the Victorian era. Her close relationship to her husband, Prince Albert, endeared her to the nation and her later role as an interested and pro-active mother and grandmother counterbalanced the nation's concerns at her German descent and her overseeing, albeit as a constitutional monarch, of a sometimes aggressively expansionist policy. In accordance with

her wishes, on her death, her body was dressed in white together with her wedding veil. Whilst black became a necessity after the death of her husband, she was determined that her own funeral would be different and left instructions for London to use purple and white decorations to celebrate her life and reign. Across the country, news of her death was proclaimed from town halls and civic buildings in late January 1901; here we see the proclamation being delivered outside the Old Town Hall in Maidenhead.

Above: The tradition of 'beating the bounds' goes back many hundreds of years although evidence of its exact origins, in Anglo Saxon times, is somewhat obscured: the Romans, Vikings and Pagan tradition have all been credited with some part in its birth and perpetuation. Traditionally, clergy included in the ceremony offered up prayers for a successful forth coming harvest and led the singing of hymns. The re-confirming of the parish boundaries generally occurred on Ascension Day and was traditionally carried out by young boys, beating the boundary markers such as rocks and other natural elements, with green branches from birch and willow trees. Young boys were chosen so that the witnesses to the position of the boundary should survive as long as possible. Actual boundary 'markers' were sometimes surreptitiously moved and 'beating the bounds' required the memory of local people in order to re-assert these boundaries. Ale and refreshments offered at its conclusion fuelled its popularity as a community event. This photograph was taken in 1908. In more modern times, as seen below in 1973, accurately surveyed records of the parish boundaries removed the necessity and legality associated with the annual 'beating of the bounds' although the tradition still exists in some places as a vital reminder of historic practices including the handing out of newly minted coins to local children.

SLOUGH, MAIDENHEAD & WINDSOR MEMORIES

Right: In 1902, the Prince of Wales Hospital in London was re-named King Edward's Hospital on the accession of the Prince to the throne after the death of his mother, Queen Victoria. The King's Fund, set up to support the work of the hospital, was founded in 1897 at the Prince's suggestion. From the second decade of the twentieth century, the Fund took up a wider remit, representing the health and welfare issues of hospitals across the country, a role which it still fulfils to this day. After the creation of the National Health Service in 1948, the role of the King's Fund altered again, with a new emphasis on research, particularly with regard to improvements in health care. In this picture taken in 1907, this procession in High Street, Slough, is part of a fundraising event to support The King's Fund.

SLOUGH, MAIDENHEAD & WINDSOR MEMORIES

Left and above: The accession of King George V and Queen Mary in 1911 was tinged with sadness at the death of George's father, King Edward VII at the age of 69, after less than ten years on the throne. With the death of Queen Victoria, Edward's mother in 1901, came the end of the rule of the House of Hanover. Victoria's husband Prince Albert was from the House of Saxe-Coburg and Gotha and so Edward became the first British monarch of the House of Saxe-Coburg and Gotha. In 1914, on the outbreak of World War I, uncomfortable questions about King George's German background caused him to relinquish all his German titles and connections. Links between European Royal families and aristocracy at the turn of the century were inevitably strong because of the tradition of marrying Royal cousins. King George's first cousins were Kaiser Wilhelm II of Germany, otherwise known as 'the enemy' and Tsar Nicholas II of Russia. In 1917, King George V changed the family name from Saxe-Coburg and Gotha, to the House of Windsor, so formalising the connection to the town of Windsor and the surrounding district. Local residents put their sadness to one side, as we can see in these pictures taken in Maidenhead and Slough in 1911. Such celebrations brought out local groups and organisations at their marching best. Every man, woman, child and dog seemed to be out in the street celebrating this event. The efforts of local businesses to outdo their neighbours with impressive flags and bunting could be seen at most Royal celebrations across the country during the twentieth century.

On the death of King George, his eldest son became Edward VIII in 1936, although he was never crowned. He infamously abdicated in December of the same year, over his intimate relationship with an American, Wallis Simpson, whom he was determined to marry, despite the consequences. King George V was eventually succeeded by his second son who was crowned King George VI in 1937.

SLOUGH, MAIDENHEAD & WINDSOR MEMORIES

When the Domesday Book was compiled at the time of William the Conqueror, several villages in the area of Slough were mentioned. Ditton, Farnham, Stoke Poges and Upton were all recorded although Slough, then called Slo, was first noted in 1196. However, the village only mushroomed into a town in the 19th and 20th centuries. Slough first became a district of local government in 1863 and in 1894 was given the title of civil parish before being recognised as an urban district the same year. More extensive boundary changes at the end of the 1930s increased the size

SLOUGH, MAIDENHEAD & WINDSOR MEMORIES

of Slough substantially. The residents of the town enjoyed four days of partying and celebration in September, 1938 as the town received its charter as a borough, the Charter Mayor took up his office and the town's coming of age was finally recognised. In the picture below, we see the new Mayor enjoying the celebrations, with a large group of young partygoers, at the Amusement Fair in Upton Court Park.

The Mayor, Edward T. Bowyer, son of a builder and himself an auctioneer and estate agent, was elected to the local council in 1912 and in 1922 he became a county councillor. He was a veritable 'man of Slough' and it was only fitting that he was elected as the Charter Mayor. He continued to be a highly respected servant of his town until his death in 1944. By the time he was installed as mayor in 1938, Slough had a population of 50,000. In the 1990s, Slough became a unitary authority. Most of the youngsters in this photograph enjoying the celebration will now be in their eighties but no doubt will still remember the dedication of Edward T. Bowyer to his town.

The procession through the streets (left) with grand, horse-drawn carriages, in celebration of the granting of the Charter, brought large crowds out onto the pavements of Slough, a true community event.
A formal part of the Charter Day celebrations was the formal shaking of the Mayor's hand (bottom left) by the Lord Lieutenant of Buckinghamshire, Lord Cottesloe, putting the seal on a great day for the Mayor and people of Slough.

SLOUGH, MAIDENHEAD & WINDSOR MEMORIES

Right: After the start of hostilities in 1939, life somehow had to go on, particularly for the children. Father Christmas has arrived at The Aspro Christmas children's party to help Mr. Mayor and Madam Mayoress to hand out presents, provided, of course, that the 'little' people are ready to be dragged screaming away from the treat of as much jelly and cake as they can eat! The promises of presents and, probably, more jelly and cakes followed by silly games that you only ever played at parties, would probably do the trick!

Below, top right and bottom right: VE Day in 1945 and the months afterwards, saw street parties across the country, as locals

SLOUGH, MAIDENHEAD & WINDSOR MEMORIES

found the will to smile again and feel the enormous relief of freedom from conflict and a togetherness from having made it to 'the other side'. The anticipation of a future, despite loss, change, destruction and uncertainty took people into a new battle against shortages, rationing and a push for jobs and a revived industrial sector. The nationalisation of the coal industry and the introduction of the National Health Service, both within three years of war ending, were the government's signal to the nation that things were moving forward – not everybody was as confident! Meantime, first of all, let's have a party! This mix of adults and children outside the Women's Institute Hall in Elmhurst Road, Langley (above), look to be having fun. At the back of their minds will be a question mark regarding the men folk and their return – or not. Relief was tempered with uncertainty and real joy could not be allowed to intrude on reality.

The party at Trafalgar Place, Old Windsor, seems a more intimate affair, with serious expressions reflecting the worry and heartache behind the mask. The predominance of women in the photograph below of a street party in Salt Hill Way, Slough in 1946, suggests that many men were still not back from fighting – and, of course, some would, sadly, never return.

SLOUGH, MAIDENHEAD & WINDSOR MEMORIES

Above: The Slough Model Flying Club display was, in the late 1940s, held at the Hawker Airfield in Langley. In this photograph, taken in 1948 or 1949, we witness a welcome visit from Queen Elizabeth the Queen Mother and her younger daughter, Princess Margaret. The late forties saw the Royal Family take on the responsibility for lifting the spirits of the country's citizens, after the worry and uncertainty of war. Their preparedness to show their faces and meet the public, on all levels, throughout the country, was their way of saying 'thank you' to everyone for standing together and resisting defeat, whatever the sacrifice.

Below: For children of a certain age, Christmas can be magical. The symbolic figure of Father Christmas has been around since the 17th century. During the war, in the early 1940s, it was important for children to know that some things would still happen and that included the arrival of Father Christmas. Children who had been evacuated, mainly out of London, away from the 'blitz' bombing of the capital, were in particular need of something familiar; so much had been taken away, so much was unfamiliar. This large group of evacuees look really happy to greet Father Christmas and his sack of goodies!

Below and top right: In the 1950s, when these photographs of Father Christmas were taken during his 'visit' to the Slough and District Co-op store, in High Street, Slough, the expectations of children at Christmas time were, by necessity, more modest than they would be today. At the end of World War II, many people were, literally, penniless. For some, there was no work and, in some cases, there had been no paid work during the war. Husbands and fathers and, occasionally daughters, had been away fighting and, if and when they had returned, they did not necessarily do so as the same person. Many were scarred mentally or physically by the rigours of warfare and, for a lot of families, massive adjustments to relationships were necessary. Difficult times often centred around the predictable expectations of familiar events such as Christmas. The sacrifices made by fighting personnel during the conflict were extreme but, on their return, these sacrifices were supplemented with more mundane shortages and obvious changes in everyday life. Adults had an acute awareness of these issues, but for children the opportunity

SLOUGH, MAIDENHEAD & WINDSOR MEMORIES

to get excited about the things that mattered to them was natural and spontaneous, but not always tempered by the reality of the moment.

A visit to any grotto, glen or palace was an exciting prospect and here we see Father Christmas looking a bit desperate for visitors – or maybe a breath of fresh air was required? Whatever the year the Slough Co-op invited him back! A visit to Father Christmas has been and should be a brief chance to indulge in fantasy and to enjoy surprises and share quality togetherness with family. The opportunity that adults and children alike desperately need as they approach this hectic time of year demands a reflective moment, a chance to 'stop the world and get off' – in this case, at the Slough and District Co-op in the High Street!

Right: Like most Royal events throughout the 20th century, both sad and glorious, the Coronation of Queen Elizabeth II was a good excuse to share the day, in this case, with a country-wide party and the extravagant decorating of public buildings, such as the Old Town Hall in Maidenhead, seen here in 1953. On the early death of her father in 1952, Princess Elizabeth, at the age of 25, became Queen Elizabeth II of the United Kingdom and of many countries and islands around the world. Although the monarch is no longer drawn, in any meaningful way, into the day to day politics of this or any other country, she still reigns over almost 130 million subjects.

As of now, she has reigned for a staggering 57 years, as did James VI over Scotland; George III ruled over Great Britain for 59 years and Queen Victoria ruled over the United Kingdom of Great Britain for 63 years; so the record is there for the taking, although Prince Charles may have other ideas – trouble is, he's already had them for a very long time!

During World War II, it was suggested that Elizabeth and her younger sister, Princess Margaret, should be evacuated to Canada, for reasons of security. In fact, the Princesses spent from 1940 to 1945 at Windsor Castle. By 1945, Elizabeth had begun to carry out solo, as opposed to family, duties and in 1947, despite some misgivings, particularly from her mother, she married Prince Philip of Greece and Denmark. She had met the Prince on at least three occasions and they had, probably, corresponded from when she was just 13.

By 1951, Elizabeth frequently stood in for her father, the King, whose health, by this time, was failing. Whilst on tour in Kenya in February 1952, the Princess was informed of his death. Before her Coronation on June 2, 1953, Elizabeth had to mourn the passing of her grandmother, Queen Mary, in March 1953.

By the time of her Coronation, Queen Elizabeth II was confident and experienced in Royal affairs and had already proved, as The Princess Elizabeth, that she had the resources and personality to successfully take up the reigns of the monarchy.

SLOUGH, MAIDENHEAD & WINDSOR MEMORIES

On 6 June, 1977, Queen Elizabeth II lit a bonfire beacon at Windsor Castle, which was echoed by the lighting of other beacons around the country, to celebrate her Silver Jubilee. On the following day, parties and celebrations were nationwide.

At a lunch in the Guildhall, in London, attended by, amongst others, all remaining Prime Ministers who had served the Queen during her reign, she renewed her pledge 'to the service of the people' which she had made on her accession to the throne. The excuse for parties and celebrations was welcomed by most of the population.

42

SLOUGH, MAIDENHEAD & WINDSOR MEMORIES

Local people naturally relished their participation in the Water Pageant (top left), held on The River Thames at Maidenhead, floating boats of every sort and kind. The participation of what we now call 'celebrities', such as Brian Johnston and boat race commentator, John Snagge (bottom left), added to the appeal for the general public. The young people of Badminton Road, Maidenhead (below), seem to be enjoying their street party even though most were not born when our monarch came to the throne. Invited to join in the celebrations, with their 'vintage' fire engine, the Maidenhead firemen (left) required little encouragement; these Queens of Beauty were obviously not celebrating their Silver Jubilee!

SLOUGH, MAIDENHEAD & WINDSOR MEMORIES

Parades included every advertising opportunity known to man and woman, although this open-top Bristol Lodekka bus (bottom right) has been put to appropriate use by the staff of Walwyns Travel Centre, reflecting as it does, consciously or unconsciously, that Queen Elizabeth II was also Queen of such exotic places as The Solomon Islands, Antigua and Barbuda, Barbados, Tuvalu, Grenada, Jamaica, etc.!

The Silver Jubilee celebrations extended to the wider district, including a 'bit of a chat' from TV personality Michael Parkinson and the attendance of the 'fairy queen', complete with wand! For the last 40 years, Michael Parkinson, his wife Mary and their three children have lived in the idyllic British village of Bray, in Maidenhead.

Michael used to frequent a pub overlooking the Thames called the Riverside and on occasions he could be seen rowing down for Sunday lunch, and by his own admission "rowing back rather erratically"

The pub is now The Waterside Inn owned by his friend Michel Roux Snr and his son Alain. It is one of the two restaurants in the village to have three Michelin Stars. The other is The Fat Duck owned by Heston Blumenthal.

SLOUGH, MAIDENHEAD & WINDSOR MEMORIES

45

FAMILY HOME
Royals in residence

On the death of his father, King Edward VII, in 1910, the accession of King George V, together with his wife Queen Mary, as the first British monarch of the House of Windsor, bound the Royal Family more closely to the towns of the region. At the hub of this relationship was the magnificent Windsor Castle, providing a convenient residence for the Royal Family outside the capital and renewing its role as a focus for visitors and a burgeoning tourist industry.

Right: This statue of Queen Victoria in Castle Hill, Windsor, was unveiled in 1887 in celebration of the Queen's Golden Jubilee. It was designed and created by Sir Edgar Boehm, a naturalised Briton of Austrian descent and an outstanding sculptor of the period. The statue was constructed 14 years before the death of Queen Victoria in 1901 and was paid for by residents from surrounding districts. Fifty years after her accession to the throne, as a slim young girl of 18, the unveiling of this statue was a fitting tribute to the affection in which she was held by her subjects and remains to this day as a reminder of the immense social, cultural and political influence she exercised, largely on behalf of the nation, as the last Queen of the House of Hanover.

The Home Park, adjacent yet separated from Great Windsor Park, included the Home Farm. Situated on the east and north sides of Windsor Castle, we see in this photograph from the early 20th century, a somewhat idyllic vista. The picture was taken roughly forty years after the modern boundaries of the Parks were defined in the 1846 Windsor Improvement Act, designed to determine access and restrictions as to their use.

SLOUGH, MAIDENHEAD & WINDSOR MEMORIES

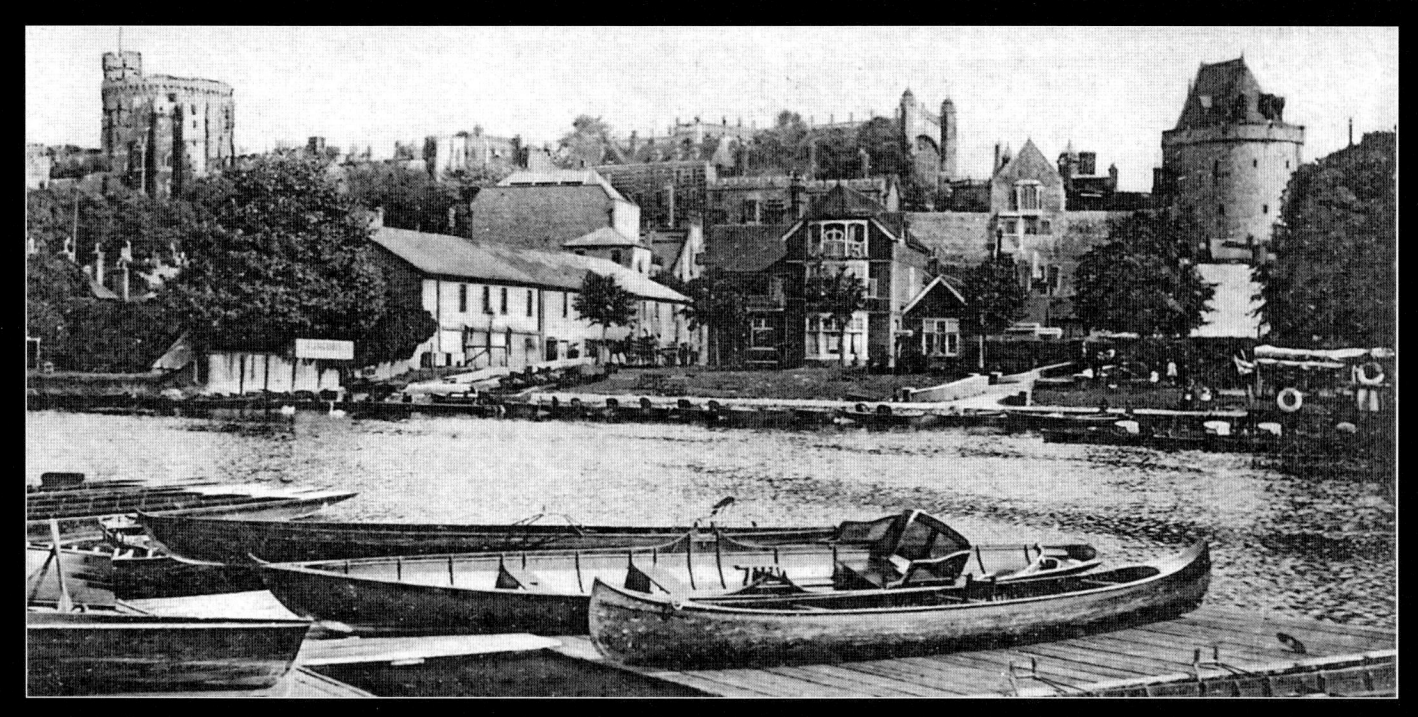

Eton College and Windsor Castle have enjoyed parallel histories, not least due to their close proximity to each other. The College was founded in 1441 by King Henry VI as "King's College of Our Lady of Eton besides Wyndsor" and remains one of the original schools defined by the Public Schools Act of 1868. Still seen as the ultimate educational goal for many monied families around the world, it has educated a total of 18 former prime ministers and approximately one third of students go on to study at Oxford or Cambridge Universities. Its proximity to the River Thames influenced the extent of its water sports and boating activity. The College itself was constructed from bricks manufactured in the brickworks at Slough. This quiet yet magnificent view of the Castle is taken from the Eton College boatyards.

SLOUGH, MAIDENHEAD & WINDSOR MEMORIES

The Royal Family and the government of the day eventually agreed that the best place for the young Princesses Elizabeth and Margaret, below, to remain safe during World War II would be Windsor Castle. Far enough away from the industrial heartland of the capital, a magnetic pull for the attention of the Luftwaffe, but near enough for their parents to make regular visits, it seemed a familiar and friendly place for them to spend the wartime years. With petrol rationed and in short supply, it made sense for the pony and cart to be put at their disposal for the duration (below); great fun, at least that's what the corgi thinks!

In recent years, many members of the Royal Family have made strenuous efforts to lead, or appear to lead, a 'normal life', whatever that may mean! For us, mere mortals, it is, perhaps, a need to recognise in our Royal Family, that fine line between the infallibility of those privileged by the historic fortune of their birth and ancestry and the fallibility of fellow human beings with a similar aptitude for weakness, failure and the visible presence of ordinary traits of human behaviour. In other words, whilst the meaning and understanding of 'respect' changes on an annual basis, we all enjoy those fleeting moments of connection displayed by various members of the Royal Family over the last hundred years. In the twentieth century, despite a generally continuous aloofness and 'otherness', many Royals extended their touch to their subjects on many occasions.

A family-owned and prestigious business such as Edward T. Biggs & Sons, in Maidenhead, selling jewellery and antiques, proved a regular haunt for

SLOUGH, MAIDENHEAD & WINDSOR MEMORIES

In the 1950s, Princess Margaret, was well-known, maybe even notorious, for wanting to get out and about, emphasising somehow that this was the pay-off for being the younger sister: a level of anonymity guaranteed as a result of the distraction by the inevitable and agreed focus on her elder sister, the monarch. Princess Margaret was well-known for doing things 'her way' and, from the mid-1950s, enjoyed a freedom rarely possible for a member of the Royal Family. Below we see her enjoying an afternoon of quality shopping with Mr. Biggs in his High Street, Maidenhead store.

Royals staying at Windsor Castle. A visit from Queen Mary in the early 1930s (above), was probably not unexpected or unusual, although by this time, her husband King George V, was suffering from continuous ill-health. Queen Mary, although of partial German extraction, had been brought up in the United Kingdom and was seen by most people as the archetypal regal consort. Originally engaged, at the age of 24, to the then heir to the throne, Prince Albert Victor, who suddenly died from pneumonia, she became engaged to his brother, who, acceded to the throne as King George V in 1910.

Individual, well-run family businesses, dealing in the more exclusive range of products, could provide a pleasant, informed and discreet opportunity for a Royal, including the monarch of the day, to take a short trip into a small and local town centre without causing too much fuss or complication. It would, however, be noted by locals and reported by the local media, and consequently cause residents to feel that their lives had been gently touched by, as it were, the 'untouchables'.

SLOUGH, MAIDENHEAD & WINDSOR MEMORIES

SLOUGH, MAIDENHEAD & WINDSOR MEMORIES

Left: Our present monarch, Queen Elizabeth II, together with her husband Prince Philip, almost pioneered the 'walkabout' incorporating remarkably close and personal contact with admiring members of the public. At times, due to the involvement of the country in a range of political or military initiatives around the globe, security has modified these opportunities, but they still remain an integral part of Royal Visits. The Queen's son, Prince Charles, has perpetuated these contacts with a strong commitment to the recognition of multi-culturalism and the further development of communities and their groups. In this photograph (left), taken in 1961, the Queen is taken on a short tour of Windsor town centre in order to appraise herself first-hand of a recent 'facelift' to the town.

Above: This 42nd birthday picture of Queen Elizabeth II, with her family, was taken in the grounds of Frogmore, Windsor, on April 21, 1968. The twentieth century saw a continually changing Royal Family in terms of their image, their relationships with the public and their response to the keenly manipulating activities of various sections of the media. When this photograph was taken the media's worst excesses were yet to come and the Royal Family, as seen here in a relatively private and tranquil moment, respectfully recorded for prosperity and the record, cannot have imagined the pain and excesses to come over the next forty years. As they ploughed their way through all the mishaps, traumas and tragedies of family life, they became, by default rather than by design, closer to the lives of any resident of your average semi. The altered profile of the monarchy now enables it to co-exist with the public in a more realistic and worldly way, generally eliciting less sensation and negative attention. The rise and rise of the somewhat depressingly ordinary world of 'celebrity' has undoubtedly cast its dark and questionable shadow over us all.

DARK DAYS
Conflict and survival

From the days of the Boer War onwards, communities around the country have provided thousands of volunteers, ready and willing to commit themselves to the defence and protection of the nation. Inevitably, the volunteering of groups of 'friends' from the community often ended, sadly, in the wiping out of whole generations in their prime. Families suffered the loss of young and old into the next generation. Conflict brought pressures on the whole population. Women, largely obliged to remain on the home front unless they were nurses or ambulance drivers, took over responsibility for the day-to-day running of the country and were often required to learn new skills to enable them to carry out previously male-dominated roles. Gender divisions became blurred by the end of World War II. The loss of so many male soldiers during the conflict meant that, in many cases, women were obliged to continue in peacetime with their wartime roles. Equally, some men returning from conflict found that there was increased competition for some of their traditional roles in the workplace.

The Boer Wars were and still are seen as a somewhat ignominious attempt at Empiric expansion. The first Boer War in 1880-81, had been a relatively short affair and the British had succumbed to the resistance of the Boer settlers in the Transvaal in southern Africa. The second Boer War was a long-drawn out and bloody affair, from 1899 to 1902, causing many people in Britain to rail against a barbarism not previously experienced. Conditions for soldiers were appalling and the introduction for the first time in military history of the 'concentration camp' and an eventual 'victory' did nothing to appease the criticism at home. The slaughter of and damage to volunteers was substantial. The photograph of returning volunteers in Maidenhead was taken around 1902.

In times of war, communications and, in particular, transport, are vital for the continued ability of the country to function. They have shown throughout history, however, including recently, that they are also extremely vulnerable to the efforts of unwanted and violent insurgents. As now, in 1914, there was an awareness of the need to maintain high levels of security at critical points in the infrastructure of the country. The photograph of an armed guard placed at the railway bridge in Maidenhead, was taken in 1914.

The Land Army focused the lives of women on something which they knew a great deal about — food! Although these are, of course, World War II Land Girls, the Women's Land Army was actually formed in 1917 as a response to food shortages during World War I. Re-formed in 1939, the Land Army found it difficult to recruit at first, not least because of increased opportunities for women in the armed forces, and by 1943 numbers were still low. By late 1944 the Land Army had 80,000 members and was not disbanded until the end of 1950. The work was hard and dirty and the hours long, but there were often great friendships amongst Land Army girls, culminating in life-long relationships. Living mainly in rural communities, in hostels or private homes, the free time options for the girls were usually local village hall dances and the occasional visit to a cinema. Their contribution to food production and land management was profound and an absolutely essential component of victory. This picture of Land Army girls was taken in the early 1940s.

World War II brought together different agencies to support the needs of the people. In Slough, a Mobile Canteen was given by the American Red Cross and manned by the Women's Voluntary Service. Such services were invaluable in the stressful daily lives that people endured during wartime. Formed in 1938, the WVS, originally called the WVS for Air Raid Precaution, changed its name again in 1939 to the WVS for Civil Defence. It became an integral part of support work during World War II, providing support to civil defence workers and the general public. Sadly, 241 WVS members died whilst on duty in World War II.

WVS appeals and distribution centres organised salvage collections for the armed forces. Aluminium pots and pans, kettles, saucepans, jelly moulds and colanders were gathered from local homes. In these photographs (below left and top right), the sorting is mainly concentrating on the toys and clothes that have been gathered. Nothing that was of possible use or that could be recycled was discarded. There were any number of appeals for clothing and toys for displaced and unfortunate families. Keeping children occupied and away from the more damaging aspects of the war was a major priority for any family.

Through the WVS, many women established a role for themselves on the home front and many continued their membership in peace time and it remains a thriving organisation throughout the country.

The role of women during World War I had caused many people to consider the potential for women in times of conflict and The Girls Training Corps was set up at the outbreak of World War II with the intention of training young girls in a variety of disciplines which would prepare them for service in the armed forces. Volunteer trainers for the Corps included some illustrious names, such as Lady Lloyd George and Lady Mountbatten.

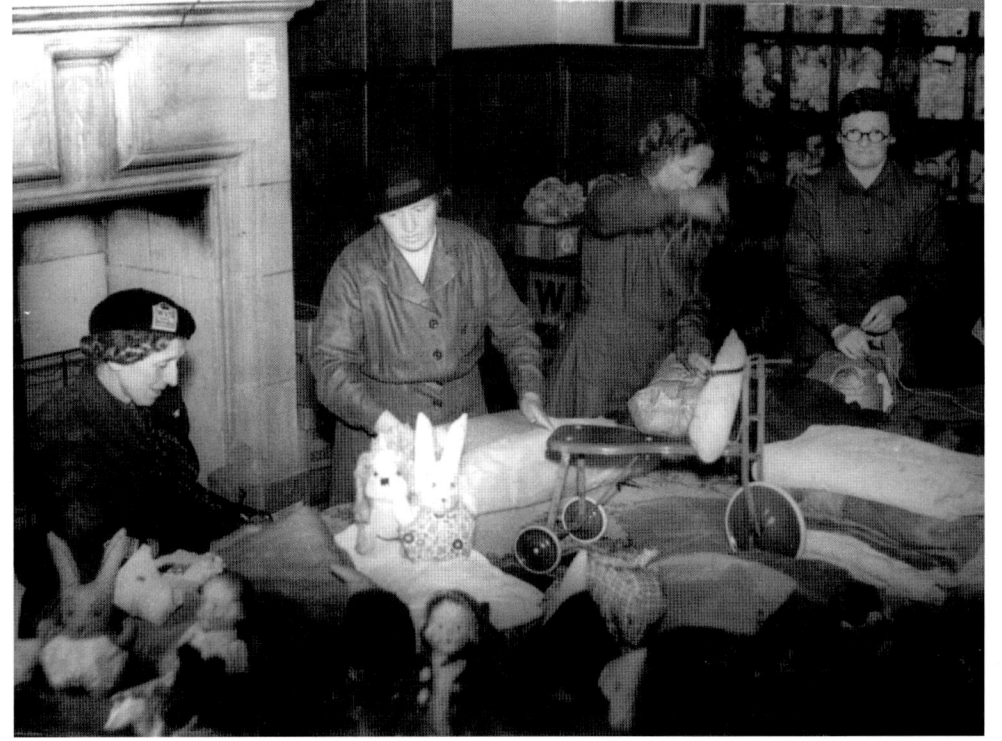

SLOUGH, MAIDENHEAD & WINDSOR MEMORIES

In World War I, women had inevitably taken over many of the traditional roles of men like never before, working in engineering factories, producing munitions and driving ambulances and trucks. Heavy manual work was not uncommon for women in order to keep communities ticking over whilst the men were at the front fighting for king and country. Many work practices and methods had to be changed or adjusted to allow processes to continue, albeit sometimes at a slower pace. Before the onset of hostilities in World War I, over a quarter of the female population was working. During the war, this number increased substantially and by the end of the conflict, people's view of what women were capable of had changed radically. Despite the trade unions of the day insisting that all women seconded to work during the war years would lose their jobs immediately the conflict came to an end, it was clear that the extended suffrage offered to women in the following years was almost entirely due to this changed view of women at work.

The scale of women's contribution during World War II increased noticeably. All women between the ages of 18 and 50 years were expected to take on an active role and by the end of 1941 an allocation system had been introduced for these women in order to place them in appropriate locations, either on the land or in factories or workshops. Many women still fulfilled traditional women's roles, such as nursing and ambulance driving. But they were now also running first aid posts, driving buses and trams and, for the first time, had more opportunities as members of the armed services. Indeed, such was the lure of these service roles for women, the Land Army became unacceptably short of volunteers at the beginning of World War II and the armed services were obliged to refuse some potential recruits so that there were enough women available to produce the nation's food.

During the war, many women had been empowered by taking on unfamiliar roles and by the end of the conflict their impact in the work place had altered forever. Precedents in some areas of work had been set or re-set, but there were some which remained for much longer. For example, for many more years to come, telephone exchange operators were invariably women, whilst, by the same token, the person who delivered our mail was invariably a man.

Over the first half of the twentieth century, the role of women had changed so substantially that their working relationship to men had to be reassessed by the end of this period. As peace resumed in 1945, relationships and family life had to be reconsidered. Some changes occurred, not through choice but through circumstances, others were necessary due to a will to change the balance of genders in the work environment and, inevitably, these often affected domestic and home life.

SLOUGH, MAIDENHEAD & WINDSOR MEMORIES

Above: This view of Mackenzie Street and High Street, Slough, has a gentle tranquillity which belies the fact that it was taken in 1940, a year into hostilities. The absence of traffic confirms the need to retain fuel stocks for essential users and the 1930s cars seen here would have to keep running well into the late 1940s and early 1950s.

Bottom: Another view, taken in 1940, of Slough High Street, again showing an understandable absence of motorised traffic and a posse of parked bicycles. The now departed Woolworths and The Eagle pub look quiet and even Boots the Chemist appears to only have a mongrel sniffing at the door. Shortages and rationing of food and fuel enforced a potentially healthier regime on the population although it probably didn't feel like it at the time.

Top right: Once more, a view from 1940, imbued with idyllic rural qualities, with no evidence of wartime activity. The problem was, that for a small petrol station such as Archer's Garage, in Dedham, few customers would be allowed to buy fuel, or could afford it and owners were likely to service and maintain their own cars to save money. Today, small village garages barely exist in a monopolised and streamlined world and neither does the service that went with them.

Below: The Hawker Aircraft Company arrived at Langley in 1936 and by 1938 had built an airfield and factory. The first production example of the Hawker Hurricane flew in 1937 powered by a Rolls Royce engine, later known as the Merlin, and was the first RAF aeroplane to be exceed 300 mph. In the first year of conflict, it shot down 1,500 enemy planes, more than the total shot down by all other fighter planes put together, including the better known Spitfire. By 1942, at the height of production, five aircraft per day were being completed, with a workforce consisting of many female workers. There were other aircraft built at Langley, including the Tempest, Typhoon, Fury and Sea Fury. By 1950, the airfield had become redundant, unable to handle the bigger new aircraft and the land was leased to the Ford Motor Company. This photograph was taken at Langley in 1945.

Right: Of Anglo-Irish origins, Field Marshal Montgomery achieved fame in his audacious leading of Allied Forces at the Battle of El Alamein, a battle which became a significant turning point in the military campaign for the Western Desert. After further distinguished service in Western Europe, including supervising the surrender of Germany, Montgomery returned to Britain. Despite his success as a commander in the field, his limited skills as a strategist provided him with a succession of posts which left him somewhat frustrated until he was invited to be Eisenhower's deputy in forming the North Atlantic Treaty Organisation's European forces in 1951. In this photograph we see him on the day in 1945 when he received the Freedom of Maidenhead from the Mayor.

NOW THEN!
Time for reflection

Each generation thinks of itself as 'modern' at every stage of life and yet we are all relics and mementos of our own history. As time goes by, we cling on to our more modish and fashionable behaviour and attitudes, sometimes with the hope that we can defy the passage of time, despite our constant creation of 'the past' and our own archaeology. In the main, we all enjoy looking back and remembering with affection things done, things achieved and comparing the context of our early lives with 'improvements' made (sometimes!) in more recent times. Things often seem not to be as good as in the 'olden days', but most of the time we are not looking at a level playing field. Perhaps inevitably, many of our childhood memories, whatever our age now, are of endless summers and snow-filled winters, a sort of 'local to us' and historically appropriate version of Dylan Thomas's 'A Child's Christmas in Wales'!

But for all of us, time marches on, and as we get older it seems strange that we find ourselves attempting to explain to our eleven-year-old god-daughter that there *was* life, of a sort, before computers, emphasising simultaneously our incredibly ancient origins!

During the last one hundred and twenty years, wartime experiences and memories have often defined generations, although in more recent times, with involvement in new conflicts, even this timeline has had to be re-defined.

Progress in radio, TV and other electronic development has outstripped most people's imagination and provided a sometimes obsessive and questionable way of 'stuffing' our days. Until the middle of the twentieth century, children had to use their imagination, inventiveness and creativity. The streets were filled with groups of children of different ages pretending to be somebody, somewhere and something else. This was fun for most, freeing and gentle in its stimulation and engendered a relevant and satisfactory competitiveness conducive to learning.

Left and below: Outside, including in the playground, improvisation was the name of the game. You didn't need a ball for a game of football – a tightly bound bundle of rags or clothes would do, with discarded jackets or pullovers for goalposts. There were games that matched the seasons, such as conkers for example; those determined to win often used tricky and dishonest ways to convert the simple conker into a hard and unyielding boulder to cheat their way to success! Later in the year it was marbles, with wonderful 'glass beads' put to aggressive and destructive use in order to determine 'top dog'. There were also 'collecting' activities, often involving cards with familiar faces, sometimes footballers, sometimes film stars. Playground games were often determined by gender, with the differences usually marked by the polarising of physical prowess and single-mindedness on the one hand and a softer camaraderie and togetherness on the other.

SLOUGH, MAIDENHEAD & WINDSOR MEMORIES

Above: In Victorian times, posed family and group photographs became very popular, even among the poorer sections of the population. In these days, fashion for boys tended to be a miniaturised approximation of their father's wardrobe, including the cloth cap for working families. The girls, by contrast, were encouraged at an early age to wear 'pretty' and bright things, generally less sober than the outfits their mothers wore. Photographs such as this, taken in the early twentieth century, also subtly emphasise the closeness of communities and the acute smallness of their world. Without personal transport, apart from a bicycle or a horse, and public transport outside towns and cities limited to the railways, life was lived and learned within a mile of home; the back yard was their district, the street was their county, their town was a foreign country and the Empire was simply theirs! – but impossible to comprehend.

Below: This picture, taken at the turn of the twentieth century, beautifully sums up that daily moment in term time when children are released from the repetition and rote of institutionalised life in school into the freedom of 'the gap' – time, geographical and social, between school and home. Change their clothes and maybe this photograph would also epitomise children of a similar age today! 'What can we do?', 'what can we get away with?' or 'what can we do that we're not allowed to do? – the eternal challenges of a potentially naughty childhood! The challenges are all there on the faces and in the body language of these children; the pretty, enigmatic and carefully turned-out and only young lady, looking wistfully into the future and already deciding that there 'must be more to life than this!'. The embarrassed disinterest and arrogance of the boys, pretending to ignore this beauty in their midst, presumably because they have not a clue as to how to change this impasse and status quo which inevitably interferes with relations between the sexes at this age. The fact that the young lady has got herself up onto the wall despite her more cumbersome clothing and that she has bagged the best position must certainly have added to the boys' discomfort: some things never change.

Above: As the relentless ambition towards personal transportation continued through the twentieth century, by the 1930s, it was still a dream for the working class, a possibility for the more thrifty in the middle class and an inevitability for the upper class. The fascination of the motor car was already forcing itself into the lives of a few fortunate children. Model cars to fit a small child were in limited circulation by the middle of the 1930s. Some were quite sophisticated in their design and construction, usually manufactured by more upmarket toy companies. Their antidote, of course, for the less affluent masses, was a more primitive 'soap box', usually built at home in the yard by dad and son, but with the advantage of light weight, a simply effective and replaceable build quality and, most importantly, greater speed!

Below right: Throughout the twentieth century, Royal events continued to be the focus of unfettered, nationwide celebration. This view of a street party from 1937 to celebrate the Jubilee of King George VI and Queen Elizabeth, has an added poignancy. Little did these children know that this would be one of the last days of celebration before the onset of hostilities in World War II. It is sad to contemplate that seven years after this happy and joyful photograph was taken, many of the older boys in the picture would be serving on the front line and maybe changing the lives of their families for ever. Typically, these boys want to be at the front of the picture, even if it means that they have to dance with each other! A photograph such as this captures the freedom and spontaneity of childhood innocence as set against the impending horror and finality of conflict.

Right: Towards the end of Queen Victoria's reign, at the turn of the twentieth century, women lived in a world of restriction and repression. They were not all unhappy all of the time but their lives were largely fashioned and ordered by men, if not husbands, then fathers. Male rules, male dominance, male control – of female lives! The First World War, or Great War as it was called, was suddenly upon the country, changing everyone's lives forever. With so many men rushing off to war, leaving girlfriends, wives and mothers behind, the order of life was disrupted and, over time, the minutiae of daily routines were increasingly dependent on women. Subjugation and subservience were not quickly forgotten but increasingly put to one side as new responsibilities were taken up, with a sensitivity and emotional response to the tougher things in life. Gender became an issue in the work place as remaining men looked on aghast as women pushed their way forward into traditional male roles, including those requiring substantial physical strength and effort. Women were soon to be seen at the heart of communities, taking a lead in ensuring that people were safe and cared for, that children continued to be educated and disruptions were kept to a minimum. Women also took on their expected roles, as nurses and ambulance drivers as well fulfilling their responsibilities as daughters, wives and mothers. At the beginning of World War I, women had little or no possibility of working near the front line, unless they were prepared and qualified to nurse. National and local charities contributed funds and goods, such as bandages,

SLOUGH, MAIDENHEAD & WINDSOR MEMORIES

basic food items, clothing and other daily necessities to a large number of War Hospital Depots which had been set up across the country. For women who had considered nursing as a wartime occupation these depots offered an alternative.

The empowerment of women during World War I carried them into a new era through the 1920s and 1930s. They had, to some extent, been liberated from the often oppressive rules left over from Victorian society. The men who returned from the war found, in many cases, a different woman waiting for them. The fashion, music and dances of the 1920s also gave women more choice, more confidence and the feeling that relationships with their men folk, at last, had an element of sharing as opposed to endurance. As the 1930s slipped by, many found it impossible to contemplate further crisis in Europe, despite the looming on the horizon, everybody's horizon, of a megalomaniac demagogue in the form of a small insignificant man determined to compensate by becoming the most evil dictator the world had known and at any cost. Women were more prepared for World War II, however, and men felt obliged to respect their abilities and potential by allowing them a greater share of responsibility in the war effort and in keeping the country ticking over. In 1940, as in this picture, ordinary yet committed teams of women went about their war work, looked after a house and family and probably did volunteer work as well. The new-found confidence of women in all aspects of their personal lives, did not, however, adequately prepare them for the social and sexual pressures that tumbled towards their loneliness and isolation. Pressured by their boyfriends to move a relationship too rapidly past the bedroom door on the suggestion that it might be the last chance to 'have fun', many women found themselves alone with pregnancy, followed by a baby, often unwanted, as they fought the prejudices of their families as well as the enemy. The emotional extremes of life in World War II were almost too much to bear for some women.

The duties carried out by female members of the Royal Family during World War II, added to the notion that women's roles had moved on and they could, when necessary, deputise more than adequately for their male counterparts.

At the end of World War II, their continued stoicism was required to learn to live with the return of a 'man of the house' so very different to the one who had walked out of the front door months or years before, as well as 'making a meal' out of rationing and shortages for years to come. For some women, born in the twilight of the nineteenth century, their whole life had been a homage to conflict, altered values and unbelievable social change. Their experience and result persuaded the next generation to push on for even greater equality.

Above: From 1900 onwards, film and cinema stimulated the wildest dreams and desires of everybody they touched; romance, adventure, danger and excitement were served up in large dark rooms, firstly with music and later with voices, as technology caught up with the idea and pushed it to new horizons. In this picture from the 1940s, the influence of actors such as Errol Flynn is blatantly obvious in a game involving bows and arrows. His playing of Robin Hood against Olivia de Havilland as Maid Marian had a ground-breaking impact for some little boys, that remained with them into their teenage years (and in some cases even longer!). Having learned, by the age of six, how to buckle their belt, it was, after all, Errol Flynn who taught them how to 'buckle their swash' and 'get the girl'! Cinema has always had an influence on children's re-enactment and performance of stories and fables. Certainly children in the 1940s rarely complained about boredom or having 'nothing to do'. They simply grasped the nettle and worked out for themselves, using their imagination, what they could turn it into and they did it together – a sort of in-house approach to everyday life!

Right: In the 1950s, toys were still quite simple, for boys and girls. The only chips in sight were the ones sat on a plate next to the fish every Friday, if you were lucky, and enhanced with salt and vinegar! In a society which still placed the emphasis on women as home makers and 'children producers', toymakers were still making a lot of money from selling pretty little dolls to pretty little girls, banking on their softness and fondness for small, defenceless creatures in their own image. This wonderful picture, taken in 1950, shows two such little girls enjoying posing for a 'family' photograph, no doubt repeated twenty years later as the 'real thing'! Note the grittily determined, no-nonsense expression of the young lady at the back and the rather shyer, slightly myopic expression of the seated young lady with hair that, possibly, she has spent the rest of her life not being able 'to do a thing with'! 'Out of the mouths of (female) babes and sucklings' came the maternal instinct, often honed through years of practice and monitored by an effective and unremitting body clock. And so it was ever thus...

Top right: For some, school days were happy days; the opportunity to be part of a team, to prepare for future adulthood by learning about ideas and theories that, when competently practised, could result in your being elected to run the country – or maybe not! Through the 1950s, classes in single sex schools, continued to protect the idea that learning without obvious distraction was the only way to learn. The downside, of course, was the ease with which some boys slipped into an instinctive and damaging bullying role, with other doubters eventually linking in out of fear for their own well-being.

Right: Once upon a time, Monday was the traditional wash day for many. For working class families, the burden fell upon Mum. Her role as a housewife meant that the day was spent boiling clothes in a tub and then wringing them out through the mangle before pegging out on the line in the back yard, or if you were very lucky, back garden. Before the days of sophisticated washing powders and rubber gloves, reddened hands were her reward and there were still beds to be made, carpets to beat and lino to wash. Later, children needed feeding and the evening meal had to be ready and on the table when dad arrived home from work. It was hard work and there were few, if any, modern electrical appliances or 'white goods' to make the task of running the home any easier. Many working class families lived in terraced housing, some of it back to back, with outdoor 'lavvies', where you learned the skill of whistling, with one foot jammed against the door in case someone else attempted to enter this small enclave of privacy. Many houses still had a tin bath that was dragged in from the yard and then filled with kettle after kettle of boiling water before family members took it in turn to soak themselves. This photograph, taken in the 1950s, shows a typical scene of what life was like in these circumstances; families and communities were close knit, sharing each other's joys and sorrows. It was quite common to lend a neighbour a helping hand in times of need. Friendships were often formed that lasted a lifetime.

Right: By the late 1950s, firmly turning our back on the gloom and shortages of wartime, the introduction and use of new materials led to the arrival of new ideas and new toys for children. This picture, taken around 1960, of a small child on a rocking horse, illustrates a modern interpretation of an age-old dream of many small children. From the days when horses were the only form of transport, little girls and boys wanted to 'do what daddy did'. Wooden rocking horses have been created over a longer period than most other toys, probably for almost 200 years, and have provided a tangible link with life over the previous century. The popularity of films set in the Wild West in the fifties probably assisted a minor renaissance in demand for toy horses.

From the 1960s onwards, toys have become more and more sophisticated, from electric models trains, accurate scale models of road vehicles of the day to that giant of practical and educational toys, Meccano and, of course, the ubiquitous and still vastly popular Lego. Over the last fifty years, more and more emphasis has been placed on the educational and learning value of toys to the extent that it is now not deemed reasonable to even refer to them as toys. The advent of simple and later more sophisticated electronic applications, largely from the rapidly expanding Far East, changed the world of toys into a more pressured and competitive environment for parents and children than ever before. Gone were the days when dad stood in his shed, cellar or back yard and fabricated out of a selection of useless left-overs, a wondrous, working and exciting replica, resembling, however vaguely, some daily artefact from the real world.

SLOUGH, MAIDENHEAD & WINDSOR MEMORIES

ABOUT TOWN
Unfinished business

Towns and cities around the country have changed massively over the last one hundred years. Changing business patterns, new technology, the need to effectively manage personal and public transport, architectural fashions, the retail explosion – all these things have enforced small or substantial and far-reaching changes upon our local environment. Whilst some iconic and familiar buildings remain, still appreciated as architectural gems and as exciting and dramatic to view today as when they were built, it is sad to note the demolition of 'new' buildings that have maybe stood for less than forty years. Already in the post World War II period of relief and austerity, the wholesale demolition of town centres began and the often thoughtless and frenzied rush for the new manifested itself in featureless and poorly designed and built structures. History is relative and 'fit for purpose' must play a part. The Listed Buildings Act and Conservation Areas introduced in the late 1960s now protect us from the worst excesses of the sometimes dubious economics of urban renewal. We are fortunate in that many of the main streets of our region's towns retain a reasonable proportion of older characterful buildings through which the history of our immediate environment can be traced and realised. Through good, and occasionally, dubious fortune, local people have been asked on a regular basis to demonstrate their adaptability, often by discarding elements of the past and by embracing the shocking and untried new. Evolution is never all 'plain sailing' and an imaginative and creative response to compromise is required from all of us.

SLOUGH, MAIDENHEAD & WINDSOR MEMORIES

Left and below: At the turn of the twentieth century, a lack of motorised personal transport made the roads as peaceful and tranquil as the view, on the left, of the main road into Maidenhead from Taplow. The picture, taken probably around 1900 at the Maidenhead end of the bridge across the river, shows horses and carts and bicycles as the only forms of transport. As, slowly, roads became more important as a means of connecting local towns, the opportunity to 'tax' people for using these roads became a reality. The photograph below, taken only a year or two later, shows the newly built toll gate and toll keeper's house.

Above: This view of Maidenhead town centre in 1906, shows again how relatively pleasant town centres were. Just like the groups of people at the back of this urban scene, you could, literally, 'pass the time of day' standing in the street! As we can see, everybody appears oblivious to the possibility of traffic, the hand and horse-drawn carts in this picture hardly constituting imminent danger. Today, it is easy for us to forget how the pace of our lives is dictated by the speed of 'street life' and its traffic.

SLOUGH, MAIDENHEAD & WINDSOR MEMORIES

Right: 1893 and the usual queue outside the Post Office! Except in this view we see mainly postmen, presumably about to start their rounds. In the foreground is the finely detailed and eye-catching facade of the Post Office in Slough High Street. It is noteworthy that many of these beautifully designed buildings from this period are not only still standing but are continuing to operate as Post Offices. It is also interesting to observe the gas street lamps of the period, long superceded but now being hurriedly re-introduced in electric form to refurbished and renovated town centres across the country. The only vehicle in view is a horse-drawn cart, possibly also used for delivering mail.

SLOUGH, MAIDENHEAD & WINDSOR MEMORIES

Left: The clothing fashion at the turn of the twentieth century demanded suits, shirts with separate and, often, upright collars, ties and a hat or cap for the men. Women wore ankle-length skirts, usually of dark and sombre colours, frilled high-neck blouses, buttoned jackets and/or long coats and hats. It appeared to men, at least, that women were, effectively, on castors, joints enabling them to turn or bend were not apparent or visible; when a woman lowered herself into a chair, it was, potentially, an exciting event for men in the room! The notion of a truly visible curve arrived only in the twenties when, through a new and different kind of music and dancing, women launched their ankles and calves on the male of the species and on the world at large. In 1910, when this photograph was taken in Castle Hill, Maidenhead, viewed from the High Street, clothes were, for women, a disguise and camouflage and designed to keep strangers as strangers. Prudery was common and expected, intimacy certainly was not! We see, again, in the photograph, the common use of the bicycle as a means of personal transport. This was possible, but not easy, for women, due to the length and bulk of their clothing. Whilst the riding of a horse had been long possible for women by adopting the so-called side-saddle, this principle could, sadly, not be applied to the bicycle. The abolition of the cross-bar on bicycles at a later date saw women suddenly able to enjoy the freedom of two wheels.

Above: The 1930s saw an increase in motorised traffic in the High Street and whilst the bicycle was still popular, pedestrians had to take a little more care when crossing to the other side. We notice, as well, that the ladies walking towards us on the left-hand pavement are enjoying a little more air around their ankles – mid-calf was about as good as it got at this time in Lower High Street, Maidenhead!

SLOUGH, MAIDENHEAD & WINDSOR MEMORIES

Above: This view of Windsor Bridge, with the Toll House in the background was taken in 1920, and provides an idea of the dominance of the Castle over Windsor town. At this time, the bridge still provided moments of quiet and stillness for those crossing over, with the temptation to linger, ponder and glance down into the gently swirling waters succumbed to by some.

Right and facing page: Here we have two views of Church Street, Windsor, one from each end of the street. The first, taken around 1920, clearly shows the ancient coaching inn, Ye King's Head. It is important to remember that, at roughly 20 miles from Central London, in the eighteenth and nineteenth centuries, our three towns had provided the necessary beds, stabling, food and drink required on the then tortuous, route to the west of England. Inns such as this, served travellers as much as they served local people.

The second photograph, taken approximately thirty years later, provides a view at a time when the motor car was, for many people, an affordable luxury, making travel to new places easier and a probability rather than a possibility.

SLOUGH, MAIDENHEAD & WINDSOR MEMORIES

SLOUGH, MAIDENHEAD & WINDSOR MEMORIES

Above: In 1930, when this view was taken, the High Street in Slough was remarkably busy. Primitive lorries and horses and carts are busy delivering goods to local businesses and babies are being transported in substantial and coachbuilt prams. At this time, the majority of shops in the High Street would have been family owned, offering the personal service that is so rare today.

Below: This picture, also from the 1930s, emphasises the functional nature of the High Street, largely unhindered by the chain stores we know so well today and with most retail businesses still reliant on the needs rather than the desires of local people. Marketing and the fashion of cultural diversity has made the High Street of today a much more colourful place.

SLOUGH, MAIDENHEAD & WINDSOR MEMORIES

Above: In every 'moral' society, the intimate experience of war and its consequences have sent people scuttling back to their prayer beads, mats and books. Religion has offered comfort and hope to many, in its varying forms, over hundreds of years. The so-called established church had to compete with the rise of non-conformist alternatives throughout the twentieth century as the lives of each individual were set in a broader context, in terms of travel, social interaction and wider possibilities. The impact of the First World War, from 1914-1918, had been enormous on the whole nation, the scale of destruction and loss of life being beyond the imagination and expectation of most people. At times like this, many people looked anew at their beliefs and faiths in their demand and need for understanding and an explanation. Non-conformist faiths grew again as their rituals were simple and seemed more in tune with ordinary people.

As we might imagine, the opening of the new Methodist Central Hall, in Slough High Street, created a great deal of interest. The photograph was taken shortly after its opening in 1932.

Left: This aerial view of the Stoke Road area of Slough taken in the 1930s, shows the housing developments which had sprung up, largely as a result of the establishment and success of the Slough Trading Estate. Whilst companies struggled across the country as a result of the recession at the end of the 1920s, Slough put itself ahead of the game, anticipating new trends and investing in the future in a way which brought new jobs, new workers and an expansive new housing development to the town.

SLOUGH, MAIDENHEAD & WINDSOR MEMORIES

Many of this country's citizens born before 1940 will remember that 1947 brought some of the worst weather conditions ever seen. Snow began to fall on Thursday, January 23, and bad weather of every sort continued, largely unabated, until well into March. 1947 gave Britain by far the worst weather of the 20th century. Conditions were exacerbated by inevitable power cuts to homes and industry from the beginning of February, following the disorganised nationalisation of the coal industry on January 1, 1947. These cuts were severe, including the suspension of 'non-essential' radio broadcasting. As the snows began to melt, so the rains fell causing widespread flooding across the country, including the Thames Valley. With most army personnel, equipment and vehicles now returned to barracks, the government mobilised them to areas where flooding was extensive enough to have disrupted normal day-to-day activity, particularly the suspension of various parts of the public transport network.

Needless to say, it was not always possible to utilise entirely appropriate vehicles to move people around. As

SLOUGH, MAIDENHEAD & WINDSOR MEMORIES

we can see, in these photographs taken in March 1947, tanks had a limited capacity for carrying people, although the young lady sitting on top of the turret is obviously hugely enjoying the experience normally reserved for service personnel. However, with their high ground clearance, caterpillar tracks and on-board equipment, such as winches, tanks and other military vehicles, for a short time at least, were able to ensure that people could get to work. As with buses, the photograph above shows that really nothing has changed – you wait for one and then three (or four) all come along together! We can also see how many local roads became rivers. In 1947, spring wasn't truly 'sprung' until April, over 30 counties south of the River Ouse having been seriously affected by continuous and heavy rainfall and the consequent flooding. The extreme and bitterly cold weather was also made worse by the disorganisation in the mining industry and the inability to get coal to where was needed. Fortunately, the years of conflict and hardship so recent in people's memories, gave everybody an appetite for survival, although by now levels of optimism were sinking to an all-time low.

SLOUGH, MAIDENHEAD & WINDSOR MEMORIES

SLOUGH, MAIDENHEAD & WINDSOR MEMORIES

In the two years after the end of World War II there was mounting dis-illusionment at the continued need for ration cards and coupons for almost everything worth having; it somehow seemed less reasonable without the adrenaline of wartime conditions. The formation of the National Coal Board at the beginning of 1947 was the start of a difficult year, with power shortages and cuts and the severest weather of the century providing cold comfort for all.

It was inevitable that the cost of being at war for six years would prevent the manufacturing industries from hitting the ground running in the late 1940s. The majority of the country's heavy manufacturing had, through necessity, been pre-occupied with making the weapons and equipment of war. Car plants, in particular, had played a major role during the conflict but come peacetime were ill-equipped to push on into the future with imaginative new designs and concepts. Because of its sheer size, weight and bulk, machinery used for manufacturing vehicles pre-war had generally been put in cold storage and was quickly unearthed from 1945 onwards in order to produce new cars, but old models, as we waited for the slow journey from austerity to prosperity. Until the 1950s, passenger cars remained resolutely black in colour and their shapes and styles were definitely 'more of the same'. In the late 1940s and early 1950s, the country was still reeling from the austerity brought on by six years of wartime conflict and remained in the grip of rationing and feeling absolutely desperate for some kind of upturn. By 1950, optimism that better times were just around the corner brought whole communities onto the streets, particularly on Saturdays, together with the need to replace some of those essential items of clothing which had, by then, been in service on a daily basis for up to twelve or fifteen years. In those days, fashion was the style you could afford rather than the fashion of the month or the season. For clothes shops, the late 1940s and early 1950s were about clearing out the old stock from pre-war days to make room for a steady flow of a more colourful post-war style that reflected the release from the worries and fears of conflict.

When this photograph was taken in Slough High Street in the late 1950s, we can see the rapid exodus away from cars in black. Initially, dull hues of grey and beige had become the new black, augmented occasionally by a dignified Midnight Blue or a British Racing Green. The other notable feature of the traffic in this street scene is that all the vehicles on view were British built and from British owned companies; how things have changed. With the now common acceptance of cars manufactured in every corner of the globe, we often forget the sheer scale of vehicle manufacturing in post-war Britain. This view displays models from Ford, The Rootes Group, Austin (shortly to become part of the British Motor Corporation and ultimately British Leyland), plus Bedford trucks and a rare and virtually coachbuilt Armstrong Siddeley Sapphire.

In the 1960s, most retailing was centred around high streets and town centres and still included substantial home furnishing shops such as Times Furnishing. With the substantial increase in commercial rents and rates and the later advent of 'edge of town' retail parks, coupled to the massive increase in personal transport, retail outlets requiring substantial floor space (including supermarkets), largely disappeared off the High Street.

SLOUGH, MAIDENHEAD & WINDSOR MEMORIES

By the 1960s, as we can see in this picture of High Street, Maidenhead, optimism had returned as everybody found their new or familiar role in rebuilding a modern and vibrant economy. By this time, fashion had moved into a new era with bright colours and new styles to attract the wage packets of those in work. We can see here the prolific economy of the British shoe industry, based largely in and around Northampton, with chain shops on every High Street. Dolcis, Curtess, K Shoes and others remained as fixtures for another twenty years or so before the emerging countries of the Far East trained and organised their lower paid labour forces to replace the market for producing and selling footwear in this country.

It was in the early sixties that the urban landscape began to change, and not always for the better. With the availability of new money, establishment of new property conglomerates and, at professional level, a desire to sweep into a new, bullish and modern era of development, many towns and cities experienced a wholesale demand for renewal at any cost. Sadly this included the thoughtless and swift demolition of fine buildings from a previous era, often still useful and useable, without a thought for the impact this removal would have on town centres and on the emotional and physical history of our urban landscapes.

Despite the best efforts of local civic societies and the national Civic Trust, these irrevocable changes occurred before the introduction, around the end of the 1960s, of the Listed Buildings Act and of Conservation Areas. Interesting to note that many of the new buildings, which replaced those put up by our Victorian forebears, have now themselves been demolished, often due to unsuitability or lack of durability. Meanwhile, many buildings which survived the purges of the early 1960s, continue to be converted to new uses which allow them to remain as visually exciting memories of what life was like for our ancestors.

SLOUGH, MAIDENHEAD & WINDSOR MEMORIES

SLOUGH, MAIDENHEAD & WINDSOR MEMORIES

NEED AND TREAT

Consuming therapy

A hundred years ago, shopping was for necessities and this was reflected in the types of shop established in the community. You went shopping if you needed something, not because you wanted it; life in those days had other priorities more directly related to family and survival.

The massive covered shopping precincts of today were preceded by the market halls of yesterday, which in turn evolved out of travelling markets set up in the fields on the outskirts of towns and villages. It is interesting to note that in some towns and cities, where market halls constructed near the beginning of the twentieth century have managed to survive the wholesale clearances of the 1960s, new covered shopping malls have been constructed and yet the old market halls continue to thrive. The strength of these long-established halls is their selection of small, family run businesses offering services and specialities not always available in branches of chain stores situated in the newer shopping centres. Whilst shopping malls and precincts across the country generally provide a wide selection of each product, they have also become largely anonymous and predictable; meanwhile, markets still retain the surprise and detail of businesses run by owners rather than by shareholders.

Department stores and supermarkets have their origins in small shops, obliged in the absence of any other retail businesses locally to stock 'almost everything'. If they were successful in business their enterprise grew and became a business with several different departments, not necessarily connected by product but by public demand.

Sadly, the evolution in the high street in recent years has seen business monopolies and commercial trends provide us with almost identical retail opportunities in every town or city we visit, with a notable absence of smaller, individual businesses providing a distinctive and unique range of products and services. The market place of the high street gives us today a massive range of products but not always with the specific product and service we would ideally prefer.

However, the high street and its attractions are still able to draw those in need of, and able to afford, regular retail therapy and will no doubt continue to do so for some considerable time.

Left: Today, we predominantly buy our vegetables in supermarkets, for the sake of convenience. We continue to do this often because they are cheaper, being purchased on such a large scale across the country. In this picture taken in Bridge Street, Maidenhead, at the turn of the twentieth century we are reminded of the fruit and vegetable shops now largely missing from our town centres. To begin with, the reference to families is quite telling, referring to life in the days when families ate fresh food together; the sign promoting 'fresh cut vegetables from our garden' indicates quite clearly the local scale of the business – no mention of factory farms here, emphasis placed on the journey from ground to table. The bicycle propped against the pavement with shopping basket attached also reflects a time when shopping more closely matched our needs rather than our desires!

Below: Again, we see another small and individual specialist shop in Bridge Street, in Maidenhead, in the early 1900s. The emporium of E. Woodhouse appears to specialise in tea, cocoa, Bovril and probably coffee. Interesting to note that all of the company names to be seen here still exist in one shape or form, which, after 100 years, suggests they have done well and been involved with a quality product. It would be interesting to know how much Twinings Tea we would have received for one shilling and sixpence in 1905!

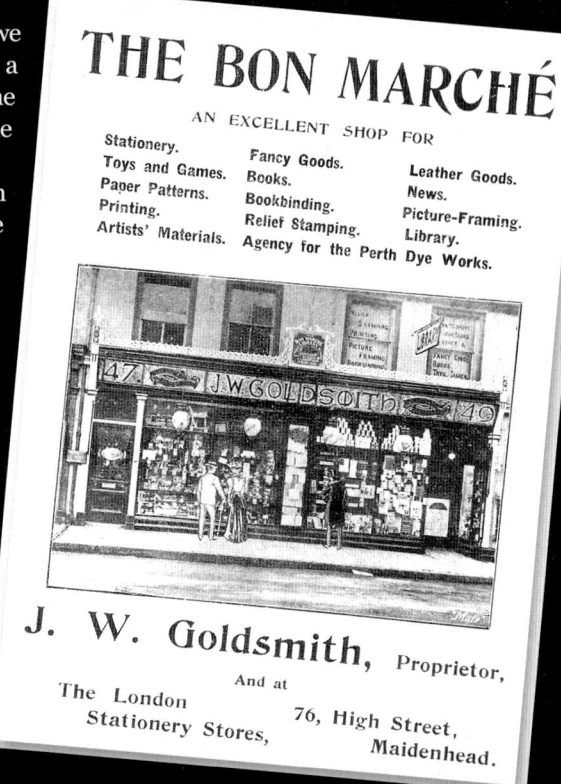

Above: J. W. Goldsmith's stationery, book and gift shop at 76 High Street, in Maidenhead, seen here in this early twentieth century advertising card, provides an extraordinary range of services to local people. Note that although books were stocked and sold, the business also incorporated a library, often referred to as a 'penny library', this being the cost of borrowing a book. Such libraries provided an essential service until the development in later times of an effective and efficient council-run library service, not least to less well-off locals who couldn't afford to buy books on a regular basis – to many they were still seen as luxuries. The advantage for a business such as this in having a library was the necessity of the borrower returning to the shop on a regular basis and consequently making other purchases. Looking at the list of goods stocked prompts us to realise how many different types of business have in later years evolved from shops such as this. Toy shops, printers, gift shops, picture framers, bookbinders, newsagents, artists materials shops, etc.

SLOUGH, MAIDENHEAD & WINDSOR MEMORIES

Above: Even today, in the few traditional butchers that remain, it is unusual for whole carcasses to be on display, as seen here in R.E.Plevey's shop in Maidenhead around 1920. The increasing speed and demands of life over the last ninety years has dictated that the well-established favourite cuts of meat are pre-cut, displayed and ready for sale. Effective modern refrigeration has also had an impact on this industry enabling 'fresh' to establish a longer connotation.

Right: One hundred years ago, manufactured foods were almost non-existent and there was a strong need to live off the 'food of the land', including local poultry. The demand for fish and birds 'without feathers' in Maidenhead can be gauged from the somewhat extreme photograph shown here. In this case, decorating a Christmas tree pales into insignificance compared with presenting your shop front every morning. Hardly surprising that they needed a ladder!

Top right: At the emporium of Mr. Arthur Upson at 35-37 High Street, Maidenhead, seen in the early twentieth century, we note again the variety of services on offer. Qualified as a dispensing chemist, Mr. Upson also employed qualified opticians and supported the photographic needs of local people. Early chemists shops often had to compete against the so-called 'quack' preparations sold by sometimes unscrupulous vendors at fairs and carnivals. In a largely under-developed medical supplies industry, desperation and suspicion sat side by side in equal measure in the minds of the public at a time when major diseases such as cholera, typhoid and smallpox were relatively common. The word 'purest' in this picture advert was there to add integrity and confidence to prospective customers. Often at this time, the phrase 'chemist by examination' could be seen on the shop facade or displayed promptly in the display window. Interestingly, in one business here, we would now have three separate businesses. Traders, like Mr. Upson, looked closely at the needs of the people and 'filled the gaps' wherever possible.

SLOUGH, MAIDENHEAD & WINDSOR MEMORIES

ARTHUR UPSON, F.S.M.C., F.I.O.,
Chemist, Optician and Photographic Dealer,

Next to the Town Hall.

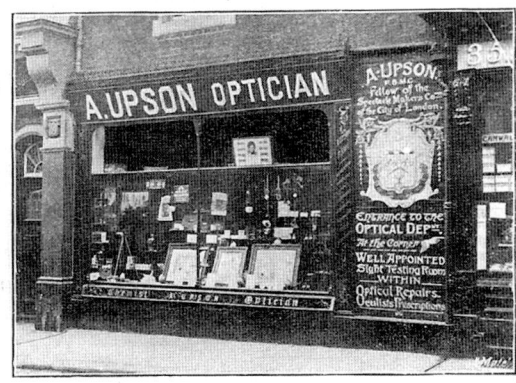

DISPENSING at Modern Prices.
Purest and Best Pharmaceutical Products all in Stock.

SCIENTIFIC SIGHT-TESTING
By Qualfied Opticians in fully equipped Private Rooms.
Consultations Free.

Amateur Photography Catered for in all its branches.

35 & 37, HIGH STREET, MAIDENHEAD.

81

Above and below: The Edward T. Biggs & Sons family jewellery business was already well-established at 32 High Street, Maidenhead in 1872. After expanding in the twentieth century to occupy adjacent properties from 26-32, the business also established a thriving trade in furnishings, travel goods and antiques, adjusting to a changed role as an up-market department store in home goods. The mounting of a large and visible clock on the outside wall of the shop for the benefit of local residents and visitors became a feature of the High Street before being moved to a bank building in the town on the closure of the store.

SLOUGH, MAIDENHEAD & WINDSOR MEMORIES

This view of Slough High Street at the junction with Church Street, taken in the early fifties, shows the buildings later to be replaced by the Queensmere Shopping Centre. and on the left we can see Milwards shoe shop, which had moved to this prime position with an eye on the future development of post-war retail shopping. Despite the date, the cars are resolutely pre-war models and all in black. Car factories had not yet returned to full peacetime operation.

Looking in depth at this photograph, we can discern that at least six of the women shown are wearing hats or headscarves, normal and polite for the period. There was always a suggestion at this time that whilst a hat was worn for show, a headscarf was worn to cover up unwashed or unprepared hair and therefore was perceived as perhaps 'a bit common' in some circles. Towards the end of the 1950s a tendency of the Queen to wear a headscarf for outdoor or sporting activity suddenly provided an aura of respectability for this small square of material and designs and materials rushed off in a new direction as fashion looked for yet another possible opportunity to swell its coffers. The clock is sited on the Leopold Institute and Public Hall, opened in 1877 and demolished in 1972.

SLOUGH, MAIDENHEAD & WINDSOR MEMORIES

Right and below: Crown Corner, in Slough High Street, gets its name from the old Crown Hotel, just out of view, apart from its sign, on the front right of this picture, taken in the mid 1950s. As the motor industry got back to production after being mothballed during World War II, the race was on to satisfy a new and rapidly increasing demand for family transport. Note the word 'family' – 'personal' transport, implying transport for each person was still not on the horizon. Yet, even with post-war fuel rationing, followed by the 1956 Suez crisis, both potentially damaging to transport demands, the rate of car ownership by the latter half of the 1950s was galloping on apace.

The left upper side of the street in the top picture was later to be dominated by the Queensmere Shopping Centre but in the mid 1950s the High Street was already becoming clogged with traffic and the need for a by-pass rose to the surface. It was, in fact, another decade before the town enjoyed the benefits of a by-pass, and in the meantime the time required to drive from one end of the High Street to the other increased year on year. For commuters experiencing the daily drag in the car in both directions along the High Street there was ample time, morning and evening, to contemplate the changing face of retail as post-war optimism and hope was converted into ambition and a new reality and acquisitiveness. We had not, at this stage, discovered phrases such as 'retail therapy' but there

SLOUGH, MAIDENHEAD & WINDSOR MEMORIES

was already a burgeoning demand for non-essentials. Our second picture, also taken at Crown Corner, in Slough High Street, reminds us that forty to fifty years ago, smokers enjoyed the 'benefit' of their own exclusive shops. The alluring suggestions offered by tobacco manufacturers of the day actually sounded witty and romantic: 'You're never alone with a Strand' conjured up the idea of a dream solution to loneliness! Addiction to tobacco was made comfortable for some by the sweet aromatic smell and for others, such as pipe smokers, by all the endless rituals associated with cutting and blending of the tobacco, with the stopping and, later, the cleaning and drying of the pipe. At the time this picture was taken, any connection between the tobacconists' shop and the chemist two doors along would be elusive for most. How things have changed.

Above the traffic lights sits a historic example of British politeness which is much less common now than then. We all know what a public convenience is but few of us referred to it as such. The loo, the lav, the toilet, the facility or, less politely, the bog, were all more commonly used, even in public. The problem today is finding a 'convenience' in a public place: if you do, it is often, either closed or a strange, out of place, metallic box looking like an escapee from a Dr. Who set! In the 1950s, there was a strong sense of propriety and public service which ensured that local councils felt obliged to deal with the most basic human crisis, and so we were never short of a public convenience.

Below: By 1958, the High Street in Slough was busy enough to cause considerable delay to public as well as private transport. The double-decker on the right is on its way to London Road with a twenty mile stretch of its journey still to go. The Bristol Lodekka was a very popular bus at the time for its versatility, its lower overall height pushing it under bridges that a normal height double decker could not contemplate. Its powerful large capacity engine and six-speed gearbox made it a fast and consistent performer over most fast A-road routes in these pre-motorway days, and Maidenhead to London Victoria would have been a typical route for this star performer.

Looking at a picture like this makes us wonder how local councils ever managed to pedestrianise large areas of their towns as traffic volumes continued to increase – but somehow, to our advantage, they did.

JOURNEY TIMES
Means to an end

Looking at photographs of roads and streets at the turn of the twentieth century we see a landscape largely devoid of all forms of traffic. If you couldn't walk, cycle, or ride a horse, or afford the cost of a carriage, you literally stayed at home. The world for most people was a very small place just a hundred years ago. With the swift development of railways and the companies that ran them as they swept across the country joining towns and cities and enabling people to see the seaside for the first time, it is easy to understand the impact this had on the landowners of the day. The resistance was considerable. Up to this time the only mode of transport across country was by horse and carriage, a sort of early un-motorised bus service. Their routes were dependent on the ability to cross the landscape and, often, the only 'developed' routes through this landscape were the better maintained tracks across tracts of land owned by the wealthy landowners. Naturally, they placed a charge or toll on all those who 'used their facility', giving them a substantial and regular extra income for a minimum outlay. The tracks and routes across their land had to be maintained to some degree by the landowners to enable them to carry out their business of 'living off the land' and the establishing of tolls to cross this land largely paid for this maintenance. Wealthy landowners had relied on horses for years and the prospect of this personal mode of transport being superceded by the very public format of rail travel, filled them with horror as did the potential loss of income from tolls as the transport system converted from horse and carriage to train. Behind the initial ruse of hiding behind the idea that their animals would be frightened by the noise and steam of trains was the fact that wealthy landowners were major investors in the creation of Turnpike Trusts which developed and constructed new highways across the country and, yet again, charged a toll for the use of these early roads and therefore needed people to use them as opposed to the railways.

In the latter part of the 19th century and the first half of the 20th century, a Royal Train was seen as essential to ensure the safe transportation of the monarch and family around the country. The Queen and her Consort, Prince Albert, had taken their first ride by train on June 13, 1842, a journey which took them from Slough to London's Paddington, prompting her Majesty to remark on the dangerous nature of such speed. This picture, taken in 1902, is an interior view of Queen Victoria's sitting room on the Royal Train; no second class here, then!

SLOUGH, MAIDENHEAD & WINDSOR MEMORIES

The photograph above, taken in 1883, shows Slough Station rail-side, with the impressive Victorian Second Empire style buildings in the background. On the other side of the buildings (below), we can admire the architecture of the designer, J.E. Banks. The station was opened in 1882

The first Slough Railway Station was opened in 1840, two years after the railway was built through the town. The delicate classical elegance of the current railway station in Slough, seen here in the late 1950s, was designed in 1882 and completed in 1884; it was re-built internally in 1938. Brunel, the famous engineer and designer of the 19th century, was the architect of an earlier rebuild of the station and the approach road leading to the station was named Brunel Way in his honour. His decision to run the Great Western Railway from London Paddington to Bristol through Slough ensured that in 1838 the first stretch of this line as far as Taplow was opened. Brunel became a hero of British engineering, despite his critics, embracing a railway from London to Cornwall, bridges such as the Tamar, countless tunnels and chunks of railway architecture, a tunnel under the Thames and the first iron ships to cross the Atlantic, all part of his portfolio.

Already, in 1904, a fleet of Great Western railway buses would have been waiting for passengers outside Slough Railway Station. After the first seventy years, the railways had done a fine job in linking major towns and cities with each other throughout Britain. The problem then was to deal with the issue of moving people speedily to the different districts in and outside town boundaries. To bank on their successful invention, the railway companies were obliged to take on the development of local transport by operating the necessary motor bus services themselves. These primitive vehicles were essentially carriages with a motor attached to the front instead of horses – but they did the job, slowly, uncomfortably but surprisingly effectively. By the early 1920s, these buses had achieved a greater level of sophistication, although with a maximum speed of 12 mph and still with solid tyres and cart suspension, this did not, in reality, suggest a great improvement in journey comfort. The picture below shows a Saloon Omnibus, built at the GWR Swindon Works, on an AEC Chassis. AEC, the Associated Equipment Company, set up in business as a bus and truck manufacturer in 1912 and under various parent companies including London Underground, the Leyland Motor Corporation and British Leyland, remained a notable manufacturer of buses and trucks until the company was sold in 1979, when manufacturing ceased.

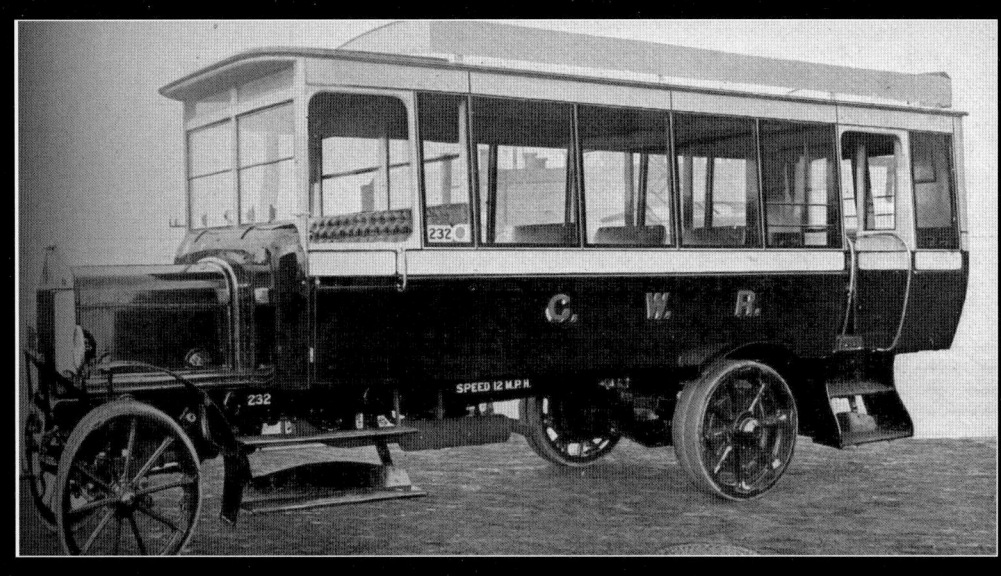

From the turn of the century, the railway companies also delivered goods from stations to local businesses, usually by horse-drawn cart. In the twenties, they introduced basic motorised lorries such as the one-ton parcel van, seen above in 1923: it was built on a Burford chassis and built by GWR in Swindon, to deliver to those local companies unable to collect goods in their own vehicles. Later, a simple 'tractor unit' with lightweight detachable trailer, ideal for use in tight places, was designed for use by the railways and manufactured by specialist companies such as Scammell and Commer. In the 1930s, horses and carts were still used by smaller businesses in towns for short distance deliveries.

SLOUGH, MAIDENHEAD & WINDSOR MEMORIES

At the end of World War I in 1918, various load-carrying vehicles became surplus to the requirements of the armed forces and were available for sale at relatively 'knock-down' prices. These were quickly snapped up by smaller businesses across the country in the absence of mass manufacture of commercial vehicles at an affordable price.

Slough Railway Station, seen bottom left in the 1950s, retains its elegance today and remains at the centre of the local community. It also remains as a reminder of the pioneering by the Great Western Railway, and its great engineer Isambard Kingdom Brunel, of a particularly wide gauge track. Acts of Parliament were passed as a controlling measure of this new and frighteningly technical form of transport. Strangely, the Great Western Act of 1835 omitted the gauge specification for the ensuing railway construction to the west of London, playing neatly into the hands of Mr. Brunel. He had expressed a wish, nay, a demand, that the Great Western Railway should develop a railway system operating on a 6ft.10ins – 7 ft gauge. Using his fertile imagination to envisage the much greater speeds which would be possible over the next fifty years and to contemplate a variety of safety, performance and comfort issues which would be more difficult, in his view, to resolve on a narrower gauge system, he chose to drive the company forward using a gauge that was two feet wider than the one laid down for every other railway company. Using an original method for laying the track and for building bridges and tunnels to accommodate his wide gauge rolling stock, Brunel developed a railway that was certainly different in concept.

The Paddington to Maidenhead section of the line was opened on the 4 of June, 1838. Despite endless difficulties with track construction and an extraordinarily unreliable fleet of steam locomotives, Brunel succeeded in bringing the Great Western Railway to a level of excellence that had been unexpected by many. This was largely due to him being, as well as an engineering genius, an intensely practical man who led his teams of workers on the ground in every project.

By 1844, the first coming together of broad and gauge railway systems occurred in Gloucester. One station with separate platforms was the solution at this stage, but time, effort and cost in trans-shipping demanded more realistic solutions. By 1850, with a preponderance of narrow gauge as opposed to broad gauge, the Great Western Railway was obliged to introduce a narrow gauge line alongside its broad gauge lines and by 1866, the first conversions of broad gauge lines to narrow gauge occurred. By 1890, virtually the complete extent of the Great Western Railway had been converted to narrow gauge. The last broad gauge engines and rolling stock had made their way to sidings in Swindon by May 21, 1892, and so ended Brunel's dream of a 'different' kind of railway system. Many of his bridges and examples of his 'railway architecture', however, survive as a testimony to the extraordinary skills and genius of the man. By 1908, it had been decided to replace many of the unreliable early locomotives, which had been converted to 'standard gauge', with more modern safer locomotives and a scrapping programme continued until 1915.

SLOUGH, MAIDENHEAD & WINDSOR MEMORIES

A GWR locomotive in full steam in 1908 (top) and a picture of the GWR 4-6-2 Pacific locomotive no.111, 'The Great Bear' (above) amply demonstrate how these great machines helped to create the idea of an 'Iron Horse' and added to the romantic and humanised notions associated with these powerful giants of the track, with their hissing, wheezing and rattling and their alluring combination of smells of smoke, oil and coal. The romance even overcame the bare reality of pollution as enormous fast-moving clouds of steam and smoke were trailed across the countryside. We are, though, reminded of their massive contribution to industrial development from 1840 until the fundamental undermining of their usefulness by a man called Beeching. It was mainly the freight-carrying lines which were axed, but Beeching's actions, together with the rapid, spread of motorways and their annexing of large chunks of the freight industry's business, served to undermine the confidence of the railway industry. The short-term response of the government of the day to respond only to the cost-cutting suggestions of Beeching, disregarding the industry's desparate need for investment, changed the rail network out of all recognition. Sadly, the freight side has still not recovered.

SLOUGH, MAIDENHEAD & WINDSOR MEMORIES

Below right: The bus on the left, destined for Streatley and photographed in 1915, was reputedly Maidenhead's first bus service; it departed from The Bear Hotel. Inevitably, these early motor buses were bone-shakers, proceeding slowly from place to place, running on wooden wheels and cart suspension.

For 300 years Ascot has been seen as a national institution. It was Queen Anne who first discovered, in 1711, an area of land within easy distance of Windsor town and Castle which she perceived, as an avid and competent horse woman, to be an ideal site for staging horse racing.

Every year, the Queen Anne Stakes is run at Ascot as a tribute to and reminder of the monarch who, effectively, established horse racing in this area. Royal patronage continuously over the centuries has ensured increasing popularity of this venue, sited on Crown property and still proudly supported by residents of this part of the Thames Valley as their local centre for racing.

Bottom: The Maidenhead to Ascot bus, popular and usually well-filled, is seen here in 1920 and was one of 23 of these vehicles previously owned by the British Automobile and Traction Company. It is a British Thorneycroft J bus, number 336 in the fleet, which was taken over in 1920 by the Thames Valley Traction Company. Still using what was, essentially, cart or carriage suspension from another age, it would still be some time before bus passengers enjoyed anything other than a jarring ride.

SLOUGH, MAIDENHEAD & WINDSOR MEMORIES

Above: One aspect of early bus design, inherited from the earliest days of the 20th century, was the unprotected outer staircase at the rear of the vehicle. For some strangely unexplained reason, this design element was still occasionally found at the beginning of World War II, as illustrated by bus number 174 of the Thames Valley fleet, seen stationary in Maidenhead in 1940. These days it would be ruled out for reasons of health and safety.

Right: How about a gentle run to the coast? - a question posed by many a mum or dad in the early 1950s at a time when the bite of post-war austerity still had fairly sharp teeth and public transport was the norm for most people. The possibility of taking a chara' to the seaside was a splendid way to cheer up the family and re-introduce them to the simple pleasures of sun, sand and water and all that they implied. Building sand castles, eating ice cream, enjoying a ride on a roundabout were available to all at Hayling Island, an island in the Solent and a relatively easy ride from our towns on the Bedford coach we see in this photograph. For 'inlanders', Hayling Island had all the family needed without it costing an arm and a leg. This Bedford OB coach was manufactured from 1939 to 1951, and was based on a small and familiar Bedford lorry, with coachbuilt bodies from companies such as Duple, and was to be seen chugging steadily up and down the roads and high streets of Britain until the early 1960s. For the more sophisticated, Hayling Island was also a popular 'pushing off' point for sailing boats and more recently became a centre for windsurfing. During World War II, the island was used for a simulated sea-borne invasion of Britain, to prepare the appropriate services for a worst-case scenario.

SLOUGH, MAIDENHEAD & WINDSOR MEMORIES

Above: In 1933, the Great Western Railway introduced a series of railcars like the one pictured here. The early versions were more rounded than this later more angular version, leading to the nickname 'flying banana'! Similar vehicles were run in many countries around Europe, mainly on quiet branch lines and in some places, particularly in Germany and Scandinavia, were referred to as 'pigs'. Amazingly, these railcars continued to be built until 1942 and ran through wartime, remaining in service until 1962 when the first British Rail DMUs (diesel multiple units) were introduced.

Below: By the early 1920s, powered flight had begun to catch the interest of the wealthy in search of excitement. It also began to interest major motor manufacturers because, of course, aeroplanes needed engines. As very experienced engine builders, having been involved, in many cases, in constructing engines for the previous twenty years, they saw it as another potential market as well as an opportunity to polish their burgeoning reputation for all things mechanical. This photograph, taken in the late 1920s, shows a 'plane from the Brooklands School of Flying, complete with instructor, preparing to taxi down the field that at this time was Maidenhead Aerodrome. One has to wonder how long the Homburg stayed in place.

Above: Upton Court playing fields have seen some action over the years but this singular event which took place in 1962 must have surprised many. Councillors, Mayor and Parks Superintendent are all here ready for the off – or were they? Perhaps it was just a 'photo opportunity', designed to promote road safety. Slough had been nominated in the mid 1950s as a typical British town, perfect for illustrating the developing issues around road traffic. After all, the 1960s were when we first saw speed traps and police with radar guns on our roads, not to mention pelican crossings and yellow lines to restrict parking. Parking meters and traffic wardens arrived to try and control the enormous increase in personal transportation. All these things are now part of the tarmac landscape and we accept them almost without question.

MAKING A LIVING
People at work

Over one hundred years, as with life generally, things have changed radically for all of us. Today, the pace of change is staggering and, for some of us, quite tough to keep up with.

Again, as with life, choices or lack of them, were what determined what we did or what we didn't or couldn't do. If we only had a horse, a bicycle or our own two feet as a means of moving around, we were limited to how far away from home we could work. Such basic considerations were common at a time when many people spent their whole lives within a mile or two of their front door. We should not underestimate the impact of families on what people did or where they went to do it. If your social life was largely contained within your family circle, you were substantially influenced by the members of that circle. You could maybe find work where your brother or sister worked or maybe your Dad's best mate knew somebody who was looking for a strong, young lad like you to learn his trade.

Where you lived had an impact on what you could do. If you lived in a coal mining area the chances were that your dad had spent years down the pit and, as his son and a fit young lad as well, the chances were that you would work down the pit, because there weren't many other jobs available and there was also the matter of family honour. The last thing you wanted as you walked down your local street was to hear "Pit not good enough for you, lad?", shouted at you by lads you'd grown up with and spent years at school with.

The changing nature of the work place in your town, would sometimes offer new opportunities and new hope. If you lived near a busy river, you might have spent some time 'messing about in boats' and thereby gained skills to apply for certain jobs working on or near the water. You may have lived in a town where a variety of opportunities existed due to the town council being forward and visionary in embracing new industries and technology at their outset. Slough is, perhaps a good example of the latter. Despite being dismissed as a backwater in earlier times, lampooned by poets as somewhere to avoid and by sitcoms as tedious and predictable, it never lost sight of the fact that it was an early staging post on journeys westwards out of London. This proximity to the capital, together with good early transport links and the voracity of its local council over several decades in investing in pioneering industrial and commercial enterprise backed up by workable social support policies, has made the town into an enviable social model followed by others.

Above: Plumbing at the turn of the 20th century was a simpler business than it is today. Without the sophisticated materials and equipment of the 21st century, it was a cruder less exact craft, reliant on materials such as lead and iron. Despite this, much of the plumbers' craft had to stand the test of time, with the last lead piping still being replaced in some older buildings today. Most water companies around the country are wrestling with the massive task of replacing Victorian sewage systems, often tackling the issue only when a burst or broken pipe forces their hand. James Head's business, at 69 High Street, in Maidenhead, enjoyed a central position in the town before the High Street was embraced by the retail trade to the exclusion of almost everything else.

James, in 1870. He was well travelled all over the globe and was known as a magnanimous philanthropist, particularly towards the local community. In 1885, he donated land and money towards the construction of a Public Hall in Slough High Street. After funding further building projects in the town, he donated land and money, in 1902, to create and build Salt Hill Playing Fields and also established a fund to pay for the maintenance of the site. He was a modest man and refused to allow the Urban District Council to name the Salt Hill Playing Fields after him. Towards the end of his life, he moved away from Slough and died in 1924. The company was eventually taken over by Horlicks in 1961 and the line continued when it came under the Beecham banner in 1970.

Above: Having established a drapery business in Slough in the mid-nineteenth century, James Elliman, Snr, started selling his own patent embrocation for all kinds of aches and pains and rheumatism, often brought on by damp housing conditions prevalent at this time. Even horses did not escape a 'rub' with this magic mixture! Production was relatively simple, using tried and tested basic ingredients. The advertising was, however, at the core of the company's business and necessitated an efficient print department, seen here in 1912. The business was established in 1847 and inherited by Elliman Snr's son, also

Below: By the 1920s, the advent of public motor transport and the increasing use of cars brought a requirement for modern, smooth roads. Road building techniques had to improve as highways became of major importance to towns keen to develop their infrastructure. Speed of construction to meet rapidly increasing demand remains essential to this day. In the 1920s, they had to do without the sophisticated digging and laying machinery we enjoy now, much of the work being down to hard, manual graft.

SLOUGH, MAIDENHEAD & WINDSOR MEMORIES

Above: The advent of the Trading Estate in Slough meant swift and essential construction of new houses for workers and the Stoke Poges Lane estate, built and shown here in the 1930s, was followed by estates of new houses at Meadfield, Manor Park, Upton Lea, Chalvey, Cippenham and Baylis Court. On the left of the picture is the Horlicks factory, famous for producing that sleep inducing blend of malted milk that became a by-word for the pre-bedtime comfort drink. The advent of the Trading Estate, spread over a massive 600 acres, changed the way people lived in Slough. Estates, such as the one shown here, all developed their own small-scale shopping areas. Personal transport was still unheard of for most working people and public transport was not always convenient for those last minute forgotten items or, indeed, for that weekly shop for a housebound mum with small children.

SLOUGH, MAIDENHEAD & WINDSOR MEMORIES

Below: The 1930s were not good times for employment in this country. The struggle to move forward with the substantial burden of debt remaining in the aftermath of the First World War, changing requirements and the slow demise of some well established industries pushed unemployment to an unacceptable level and imposed real hardship on families across the land. With the establishment of the Trading Estate in 1926, Slough had made a crucial and timely decision to invest in an organised approach to attract new business to the area. With this Estate well-established by the early 1930s, the prospects for those ready and able to work in the area was much improved. In 1936, against the backdrop of the historic Jarrow March on London, a mere 20 miles to the east of Slough, the town was relatively prosperous. Our photograph of the High Street taken at this time shows, in the right hand corner, the Ministry of Labour Employment Exchange where jobs were certainly available. Later replaced by a shopping centre, this section of the High Street was 'buzzing' in the early to mid-1930s. Just looking at the cars in this scene, we see not your typical 'family runabout' of the day, but stylish, substantial and expensive up-market saloons and coupes, suggesting that life, for some, was not that bad. As new houses were built on new estates all around the town, people were spending their money on new furniture, clothes, jewellery and things for the home from a variety of quality shops such as Edward T. Biggs. When customer service was how you stayed in business in the retail trade, there were lots of working opportunities in High Street, Slough.

Further along on the right hand side of the street we can see the clock on the Leopold Institute and Public Hall, opened in December 1877 by the Duchess of Albany, the widow of Prince Leopold, the youngest son of Queen Victoria after whom it was named. The building and its clock remained a notable part of High Street architecture until it was demolished in 1972.

SLOUGH, MAIDENHEAD & WINDSOR MEMORIES

Bottom left: The Slough & District Co-operative Society had a troubled birth. Originally, under the title of the Windsor Co-operative Society, a branch was opened in Slough in 1866. This first effort ended in failure and it was only twenty five years later, in 1891, that a second attempt culminated in the opening of the Slough & District Co-operative Society's first shop on Slough High Street, in 1892. As a basic ingredient for most kitchens, the Co-op sold vast quantities of milk, produced locally. In 1930, Slough Co-op opened a new dairy in Chalvey. Obviously, from this picture, we can surmise that the locals thought the new dairy was a 'good thing', no doubt from the point of view of better supply and possibly also for increased employment opportunities.

Above: In 1926, on the site of a First World War vehicle repair depot, in Cippenham, a village on the edge of Slough, a group of businessman formed the Slough Trading Company, later to become the Slough Trading Estate. This was the first recognised trading estate to be established in the world. The Trading Estate quickly attracted a range of companies to the site and, despite the economic recession which hit the western world at the end of the 1920s, it was almost the only part of the country that had jobs to spare. Inevitably the village of Cippenham was integrated into the Slough boundaries. The community ballooned in size and demanded all the means to sustain daily life. This photograph shows the staff and premises of the Cippenham branch of the Slough & District Co-operative Society in the early 1930s.

Above: Yet another famous brand name hailing from a factory on the Slough Trading Estate. 4711 Vanishing Cream was an extremely well-known product of the day, when this picture was taken in the 1930s, fulfilling a need for new sophisticated cosmetics in response to those perfect faces and bodies seen on the silver screen. By this time these film stars had been talking and in colour for going on twenty years. Today, cosmetics have become an aggressive and sophisticated division of a more manipulative and highly promoted fashion industry, an industry that takes few prisoners and offers less than

SLOUGH, MAIDENHEAD & WINDSOR MEMORIES

a few hundred per cent guarantees of perfection. For every ten products bought today with our relatively greater wealth, back in the 1930s maybe one product would have had to suffice. Certainly the encouragement to mirror the efforts and successes of the stars of the silver screen was apparent and they had become role models for women of the day with personal and professional ambitions.

Above: Having produced the first Citroen car in France, in 1919, Andre Citroen established a factory in Slough in 1926 to build right hand drive vehicles. In the early 1920s, Citroen had become the most popular imported car in Britain and it made sense to fulfil the demand in Britain from a local factory. The building of cars here continued until 1966. Models built at Slough were all right hand drive and, as well as supplying the British market, were also exported to other right hand drive destinations around the world. For a time, Citroen Cars in Slough was one of the largest car assembly plants in the United Kingdom.

The Citroen Traction Avant, introduced in 1934, although not the first front wheel drive production car, was the most successful. Despite this, its introduction coincided with Andre Citroen overstretching himself, with the company slipping towards bankruptcy. Fortunately, it was rescued by another highly respected French company, the tyre maker Michelin, which bought the parent company and ran it successfully until 1974, when Citroen teamed up with Peugeot.

Below: Although, still perhaps a little biased towards women in its content, the bathroom cabinet plays host to a whole range of specialist products for men. Back in the 1930s, when this photograph was taken of female workers at the Northam Warren manufacturing facility, in Slough, the perfumes and deodorants produced were exclusively for women, who, of course, did not sweat but merely perspired: by the twentieth century, perfumes were used to enhance as opposed to cover up. Twenty years earlier, during World War I, women often found themselves confronted with heavy manual tasks, and working practices were changed to allow processes to continue, albeit at a slower pace. Before then, a quarter of the female population was working, but with so many men fighting in the war this number increased substantially. Women took men's roles and by the end of the conflict had changed the nation's view of what women were capable of. Although the trade unions of the day insisted that women seconded to work during the conflict would lose their jobs at the end of hostilities, the extended suffrage offered to women in the following years was almost entirely as a result of this changed view of women at work.

Right: A genderised view of the workplace remained until World War II. During the war attitudes began to change as more women were allowed to take an active role in the armed forces. Yet again, women took the place of men in an even wider variety of jobs, simply on the basis that there was no alternative. There had still been, prior to hostilities, clearly defined areas of work deemed appropriate for women and other areas more typically fulfilled by men. The experience of women during the war doing unfamiliar and challenging work had an empowering effect. However, although 7.2 million women were in work during the war, this figure quickly dropped by over 20% by summer 1946. As this photograph taken in 1950 shows, some precedents were harder to break; the telephone operator was invariably a woman, whilst the person delivering the post was invariably a man. It took many more years for these stereotypes to change.

SLOUGH, MAIDENHEAD & WINDSOR MEMORIES

SLOUGH, MAIDENHEAD & WINDSOR MEMORIES

SLOUGH, MAIDENHEAD & WINDSOR MEMORIES

Left, above and below: Throughout the history of mankind, fire has exercised a fearful fascination. It haunts us throughout our lives as a dangerous and unremitting source of damage, difficult to tame or extinguish. Thankfully, there are those who have trained to protect us from the worst implications of fire. In 1929, the whole street turned out to watch the efforts of the brave firemen as they tackle what turned out to be a minor fire in the upper storey of The Old Crown Hotel, in Slough. Fires in towns and cities are obviously hazardous to deal with due to the closeness of other buildings and greater concentration of people. The need for the fire brigade to reach a fire quickly is as paramount today as it was eighty years ago, the difference being the relative lack of traffic in the 1930s. In the top right picture we see the first motorised fire engine of Maidenhead Fire Brigade outside Park Street Fire Station. We can quite clearly see the primitive nature of their equipment and vehicle.

In more recent times fire engines began to carry large volumes of water on board to begin dousing the fire as soon as they arrive, rather than having to wait until the hydrant is found and the hoses connected. Although modern fire engines are extremely powerful, often with turbocharged, large capacity engines, they are also extremely difficult to drive when fully laden with water, particularly when taking bends at speed: so yet another reason to admire these professionals. It is interesting to note that in some European countries, firemen, particularly in rural areas, are not employed but are volunteers.

Above: Women were, of course, very much in evidence in offices in the 1950s. This view taken in the offices of well-known Slough company, Flexello, shows that, by today's standards, life at work was relatively primitive. Chairs were non-adjustable and not even on wheels and all written communication was done with large and cumbersome typewriters rather than computers. Dress was more sober, with women in skirts and all men in suits, a formality in the work place which is not so apparent today. Chauvinism, sexism, racism and ageism existed then as they still do today, but then they were rarely questioned, let alone challenged. It was easier then to see who would make it up the ladder, who would end up with the prize. There was a greater predictability about the way the workplace operated but this also made it feel more secure for some. Work, employment and prospects were a comfort zone in the 1950s and 'isms' were not necessarily a hindrance to wanting to get up every morning and to look forward to spending the day at work. Slough has long enjoyed a challenging and successful commercial life and, applying a creative and intuitive response to new concepts and new inventions, the town has been able to put itself at the pointed end of the stick and has reaped the rewards, which have benefitted the whole area.

GEA Barr-Rosin Ltd - Dried and Tested

Relatively few local folk will know of GEA Barr-Rosin Inc, based in Boisbriand, Quebec, in Canada. Nor will many be familiar with GEA Barr-Rosin (USA) Inc. based in St. Charles, Illinois.

Those North American addresses may be unfamiliar to most people, but large numbers will have heard of GEA Barr-Rosin Ltd, a local company whose base is at 48, Bell Street, Maidenhead.

As a leading supplier of airstream drying systems, GEA Barr-Rosin Ltd offers a choice of dryers to dry a full range of wet materials, from granules, cakes and powders to sludges, slurries and solutions. The dry products can be in the form of powders, granules or pellets. Coolers and calciners are also supplied.

In their early days the company's corporate predecessors were pioneers at a time when virtually no competition existed; business was good and easy to come by. Over the following decades however, competition strengthened, forcing the business to evolve in a fiercely competitive environment. Several competing companies have failed, yet GEA Barr-Rosin has grown and become stronger as the years have passed.

Combining over one hundred years of drying experience, the company offers its customers a complete service with proven systems and innovative solutions in response to their drying needs. For decades two companies, Barr & Murphy and Rosin Engineering, specialised in Thermal Process Systems for the Food, Chemical and Polymer industries. Now united within the GEA Group, the combined experience gained from building thousands of installations is available to every client in its advanced drying and processing systems.

The importance of industrial drying equipment is something seldom realised outside its industrial applications. Yet dryers contribute to the production of countless everyday products: the sugar in our tea, the toothpaste we use to clean our teeth, the powders we use to wash our cloths, the paper we write on and the cars we drive... the list is endless.

Above left: *GEA Barr-Rosin's 48, Bell Street, Maidenhead, premises.* **Below:** *Rosin Engineering's old Stourbridge pilot plant.* **Bottom:** *GEA Barr-Rosin's Montreal office.*

SLOUGH, MAIDENHEAD & WINDSOR MEMORIES

Rosin Engineering

Sebastian Rosin started Rosin Engineering Company Limited in September 1959 to exploit his father's invention of the pneumatic dryer, which Dr P.O. Rosin had invented in 1929. The company would also commercialise Seb's own invention of a novel 'drop forming' process for molten chemicals.

A pneumatic dryer in its simplest form is a drying system where a wet granule powder or slurry is dispersed into a stream of hot gases for very rapid drying. The dried product is then separated from the air stream by various devices.

In 1963 'REC' received its first order for a large coal drying installation handling thirty tons of coal per hour from the National Coal Board. That 'turnkey' installation, including foundations and building, was the first of many such orders from the NCB.

Though London remained the base for the technical sales and head office for the company, REC opened a design office in Birmingham in 1964.

Up until 1966 all equipment was designed in-house and subcontracted to local manufacturers. REC then purchased a two-acre factory site in Stourbridge 12 miles to the west of Birmingham. The single fabrication

Top left: Mr Sebastian Rosin. ***Above:*** *A view inside the Rosin pilot plant and testing facilities. Data gained from the plant enabled the company to put forward the best design for the drier related to the most economical operating conditions.* ***Below:*** *A thermal drier installed at Manvers central coal preparation plant to serve four collieries.*

SLOUGH, MAIDENHEAD & WINDSOR MEMORIES

shop served an immediate purpose which was to fabricate two large fluid bed coolers in aluminium for ICI to cool ammonium nitrate fertilizer. REC expanded the Stourbridge works over the years, and built an office block which became needed as the company grew, enabling the transfer of the Birmingham offices. From then on all REC equipment was manufactured in-house.

By the 1970s the company had established itself as the No.1 supplier of coal driers to the NCB. REC had also developed a two-stage pneumatic system to pre-heat coking coal for coke ovens to 220°C degrees. As coke is an essential ingredient of steelmaking these plants were sold to British Steel and to ISCOR in South Africa. A two tons per hour pilot plant was initially supplied to the British Coke Research Association. The ISCOR order, through the Simon Carves engineering contractor, was for two plants each having a capacity of 80 tons per hour - a daunting prospect.

It was also in the late sixties, and in the seventies, that the company started to realise its potential in the food industry - specifically in the production of starch from maize/corn, wheat, barley and potatoes.

Starch and many of its by-products, like residual fibre and gluten (protein), need to be dried, mostly in pneumatic dryers.

Meanwhile REC also developed a large range of fluid bed processors and fluid bed polyester chip crystallisers and column dryers.

Polyester chips have to be dried to a phenomenal degree of dryness - 30 parts per million - so that they can be spun into fine filaments.

Several hundred of these units were sold worldwide: at least a hundred in China alone.

In 1980 what would become the company's 'Atritor' division was acquired from the Receiver of Alfred Herbert in Coventry. Atritor Limited had offices, a machine shop and foundry in Coventry. The number of employees in the group jumped from 100 to 150. Atritor manufactures a range of dryer pulverisers, mills and micronisers.

Top: A selection of thermal processing systems. Some of the largest drying and cooling systems ever installed were manufactured by Rosin Engineers. *Left:* A combined hoverbed drier and cooler. *Above:* A drying plant for smokeless fuel for Kersley Colliery.

SLOUGH, MAIDENHEAD & WINDSOR MEMORIES

Three years later a client who had several of the company's dryers gave it a first order for a Wheat Gluten Ring Dryer. REC designed a novel and revolutionary feed mechanism in the form of a 'fish tail' for injecting the wheat gluten, which is like wet chewing gum, as a thin film into the dryer. Dried wheat gluten is used to enhance the protein content of flour for the baking industry.

That installation was such a success that numerous orders followed from all over the world, including Australia and America.

REC was already manufacturing rotary drum dryers and coolers, but this line of equipment was given a considerable boost in February 1987 when Barrie Mathews joined the company. Barrie came from Newell Dunford Ltd and was a leading expert in the design of this type of equipment. To this day, Barrie continues to lead the company's Rotary Dryer activities.

In 1990 Rosin Americas Limited was formed with an office in Montreal to serve the American and Canadian markets.

The company was honoured in 1994 to receive the Queen's Award for Export Achievements.

As a result of such worldwide trading it became obvious to the shareholders that the best future for the company and its employees was with an internationally strong company in a similar line of business. Such a partner was the Danish firm Niro, part of the GEA group. In September 1994 Niro purchased REC and its land and factory at Stourbridge, but did not acquire Atritor Limited.

Top left: *A proud day for Rosin Engineering as staff and the Mayor gather for the presentation of the Queen's Award for Export Achievement in 1994.* **Above left and top right:** *Sebastian Rosin receiving the Queen's Award, pictured top right.* **Below:** *Rosin Engineering's former Lye (Stourbridge) workshop and offices.*

SLOUGH, MAIDENHEAD & WINDSOR MEMORIES

Barr & Murphy

Dr Peter Barr worked in the early 1930s in the evaporator and spray dryer department of Lurgi GmbH and in 1935 published his Doctor's Thesis on drop formation from centrifugal atomisers. In 1940, while studying the effect of jet ejectors in evaporators, he came up with the idea of applying the same principle of pneumatic dryers and from this idea developed the Ring dryer which was patented in 1942.

Before 1962 Dr Peter Barr had headed up the Industrial Drying Department (IDD) of F.W. Berk & Co. Ltd, principally a chemical company, but with a small engineering division. In the previous 20 years he had built up a prosperous business with a team of 12 people building drying systems for the chemical, starch and dairy industries.

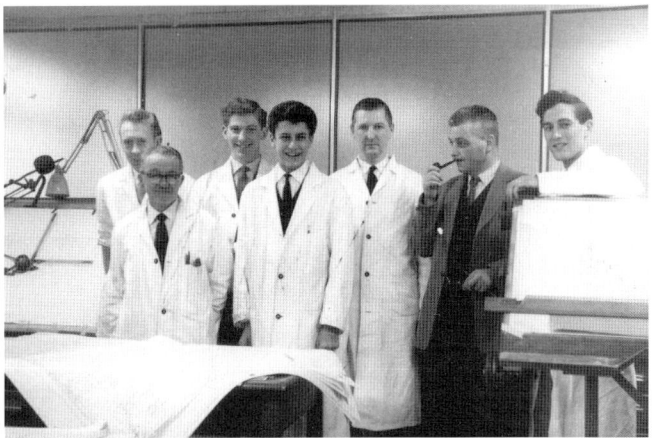

In 1962 the management of FW Berk retired as a group and a younger generation of the Berk family took over the board. They were keen to reorganise, and decided that as a chemical company they no longer needed their engineering divisions. Peter Barr and the IDD Manager, Beverley Murphy, left the company, and the rest of the Industrial Dryer Division came with them to start Barr & Murphy Ltd. At the time, ICI was in negotiation for a key order, and it decided to 'go with the brains' and order the dryer from the fledgling company.

Barr & Murphy Ltd was incorporated in 1963 with an office in Dorset Square, London. It had a flying start thanks to the order from ICI. Dr Barr had also recently sold his first dryer to the American Corn Starch Industry, and the new company was able to build on that success. The FW Berk American agent, however, did not want to work for the new company and risk trouble with Berk, but he introduced Barr & Murphy to Roland Calhoun, starting a relationship that was to last for another fifteen years and see the company become the leading dryer supplier to the American Corn Processing Industry.

Derek Barr, son of Dr Peter Barr, graduated in 1966 and immediately joined the B&M team. The American business was booming and the large flash dryers being built for the Corn Starch Industry were changing the skylines of many Midwestern towns.

In the early 1970s the American Corn Starch Industry was booming, and B&M benefited greatly from this. At the same time the Wheat Starch Industry was beginning to expand, with increasing use of wheat gluten to reinforce European flours for high volume bread manufacture. B&M had developed a novel drying technology for this difficult product, and its first sale was to an innovative producer in Germany. This was the beginning of the wheat starch boom that became the backbone of the firm's business in the late 1970s and 1980s.

*Top: Dr Peter Barr and Mr Beverley Murphy. **Left:** The Drawing Office at F.W. Berk & Co. Ltd, 1962. **Below:** One of the group research laboratories.*

SLOUGH, MAIDENHEAD & WINDSOR MEMORIES

The company was awarded the Queen's Award for Export Achievement in 1976.

In 1978 B&M had its first contact with the Australian Wheat Starch market. David Willis of Bunge visited a plant in Holland to see the process for a proposed B&M plant in Australia. Over dinner that evening a new wheat starch collaboration was born.

B&M made its first sale of complete wheat starch processing lines process to Allied

However, it was not all plain sailing. National strikes in 1972 led to power cuts and the 'three-day week'. The company overcame those challenges by using car batteries connected to strip lights, and Gaz Camping Lights for light, and paraffin heaters for the office, all to ensure that work could continue with the least possible disruption, and that no customer was ever let down.

Derek Barr became a director of the company in 1974. He founded B&M Canada in Montreal, initially as a service company for North America though later it became a full North American supply company. As well as its work in the American Corn Starch Industry, Barr & Murphy now started to explore the North American chemical industry and distilleries.

Top left: *A 1957 photograph of H.M. Queen Elizabeth the Queen Mother unveiling the plaque at No1 Dorset Square, London, NW1, home of Barr & Murphy Ltd from 1970-1986. This building had been the headquarters of Special Operations Executive's Free French (RF) section during the Second World War. Many French agents, including Jean Moulin and Pierre Brossolette, and their British colleagues in RF section such as Wing-Commander Yeo-Thomas and Captain Desmond Hubble, were briefed at 1 Dorset Square before being sent behind enemy lines. The plaque outside the building commemorates the brave people who left for missions in France and, in particular, the agents who did not return.* **Left:** *Dr Peter Barr receives the Queen's Award from the Lord Lieutenant in 1976.* **Above:** *Staff at the Queen's Award lunch.* **Below:** *A Barr & Murphy exhibition stand at a Powder Bulk Show in 1994.*

Meanwhile the Wheat Starch Industry in Europe was starting to expand, and B&M was the primary supplier of dryers for the new and expanding plants. It initiated a co-operation with Tenstar Products for its first wheat gluten plant for Miles Israel Ltd.

SLOUGH, MAIDENHEAD & WINDSOR MEMORIES

Mills and Bunge Australia in 1979. These were successful installations and saw the company take a dominant position in the Australian market expansion.

The 1980s saw the company continue to be successful in the sales of drying systems to the Corn Starch Industry in North America, but the biggest success was in the wheat starch industry in Europe, Australia and elsewhere. Barr & Murphy developed from a dryer company into a small specialised process contractor and built a number of complete process plants for Wheat Starch around Europe and Australia, and even in China. In 1989 it bought the first unit in a new development in Bell Street, Maidenhead, which is still the office base today. Both the UK company and the company in Canada had a steadily growing business.

In 1994 GEA acquired B&M's principal European competitor Rosin Engineering. GEA soon realised that if it could bring Rosin and B&M together it would have an extremely strong position in the agri-business area, and at the same time could transfer B&M's wheat processing capability to another of its divisions.

GEA made an approach to B&M in 1995 and in 1996 the acquisition was completed. After some initial teething problems the merger between B&M and Rosin was highly successful and GEA Barr-Rosin was born.

From 1989 until present, the Bell St, Maidenhead, address has remained as the main sales, project engineering and design centre in the UK, with approximately 50 staff based there and around 70 in North America.

GEA Barr-Rosin Ltd has a research and development centre located in St Peter's Road, Maidenhead, with a similar facility in Montreal.

The offices at Lye, West Midlands, were gradually reduced and final closure was in 2001. Proposals are now in place to expand the Bell St address into the adjoining unit. A similar size office unit and test facility is still located in Montreal handling all of the American business and with a sales office located in Chicago.

Top left and top right: *Views from Barr & Murphy, Montreal.* **Above:** *GEA Barr-Rosin's test centre in St Peter's Road, Maidenhead.* **Left:** *A corn starch ring duct during fabrication at Cordwallis Street, Maidenhead.*

SLOUGH, MAIDENHEAD & WINDSOR MEMORIES

GEA

Since July 2005 the GEA group has been operating under the name of GEA Group Aktiengesellschaft.

GEA stands for Global Engineering Alliance, a name which underlines the fact that the company is a multinational technology group.

GEA Group Aktiengesellschaft, headquartered in Bochum, Germany, and listed on the MDAX stock index, is a globally successful technology group with more than 250 companies in 50 countries. GEA Group employs more than 20,000 people generating sales of EUR 5 billion. The company focuses on specialty mechanical engineering - especially process engineering and equipment - and is one of the world's market and technology leaders in 90 per cent of its businesses.

GEA Process Engineering develops, designs and sells production plants for the dairy, brewery, food and chemical industries. With sales of more than EUR 1 billion and approx. 4,000 employees working in more than 40 countries, GEA Process Engineering is recognised as a world leader within industrial drying with liquid processing, concentration, drying and aseptic packaging as our core technologies. GEA Process Engineering is part of GEA Group, headquartered in Germany.

Today, GEA Barr-Rosin Ltd, led by Managing Director Ilija Aprcovic, who began his career with B&M in 1984, is just as committed to development and progress as its founders were half a century ago.

The company's declared aim is 'To be the recognised leader in the supply of pneumatic drying systems through the continuous development of innovative technologies.'

Technology is not everything, however. GEA Barr-Rosin Ltd's philosophy is to ensure that its clients are completely satisfied with the systems they buy, regardless of their complexity. Clients rely on the company's systems to operate their businesses – and with drying systems expected to perform for 30 years or more clients can be assured that they can call on the company at any time for technical support. There can be no greater endorsement than that provided by Bisto Gravy, which is dried on equipment supplied by the firm, and which is still maintained by Barr-Rosin after more than 50 years in use.

Truly dried and tested!

Top left and inset: *A rotary dryer with pneumatic exhaust and a typical rotary dryer internal (inset).* ***Left:*** *Airstream drying systems.* ***Below:*** *Wheat starch and gluten dryers for a plant in Germany.*

111

ICI Paints/AkzoNobel - 'They Know the Colours that Go'

One of the most readily recognised trade names in the world is Dulux. Today the Dulux brand of paints is manufactured by AkzoNobel which acquired ICI in January 2008.

Based in Amsterdam, and tracing its corporate history back to 1777, AkzoNobel makes and supplies a wide range of paints, coatings and specialty chemicals such as the internationally noted Sikkens brand.

Today, AkzoNobel Decorative Paints UK, Ireland and South Africa has its headquarters in Slough and employs around 3,000 people. Annual production of its famous Dulux paint would cover the entire surface of the Isle of Wight four times over.

It was in 1919, at the end of the First World War, and long before the days of DIY, non-drip paints and the Dulux dog, that the long-established varnish maker Naylor Brothers set up a factory in Slough on a 30-acre site former brickfield which had previously been used for the American Corps of Engineers' stores.

Meanwhile, in Stowmarket, research was in progress, inspired by work carried out in the USA by Du Pont; its objective was to develop new processes and finishes for use by the British motor vehicle industry. In due course a nitrocellulose finishing process came onto the market, developed by Nobel Chemical Finishes Limited and marketed as Belco.

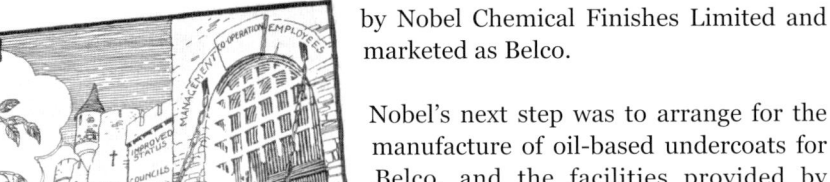

Nobel's next step was to arrange for the manufacture of oil-based undercoats for Belco, and the facilities provided by Naylor Brothers' site in Slough were ideal. Nobel Chemical Finishes ultimately purchased Naylors, and 1926 saw the start of a decade of consolidation, with the two companies working together to overcome the difficult economic climate of Britain's industrial depression.

Substantial investment was committed to research; and in the autumn of 1929 they produced a one-bake undercoat for the motor industry, the factory's first alkyd-based product, followed in 1931 by the first of the Dulux alkyd-based synthetic finishes, again based on the Du Pont formulation.

Above: The cover of ICI's first house journal in 1928. *Below left:* A training session at Slough Technical Service Station. *Below:* Testing in the 1950s.

Dulux paint was first sold to the building trade in 1932, and was met with some suspicion because it was so obviously different from the lead-based paints to which decorators were accustomed. It was thinner, went further, and dried more quickly. It was also much more durable, but although this last fact was known in theory, decorators, being practical people, were reluctant to believe it. Fortunately, architects and specifiers were more disposed to place their faith in theory, so the decorators whom they contracted were compelled to use the new product, and Dulux was able to begin proving itself. By 1939 it was being stocked by a small but growing number of merchants.

The Slough factory also entered into a licensing agreement with the American Paint Company in the early 1930s. Increased production brought problems of a new and threatening nature; records from the mid-30s give details of a controversy which almost put an end to paint manufacture at Slough. Market gardeners to the windward side of the factory complained about fumes, and the matter was further exacerbated when the Council built a housing estate on the northern boundary of the works.

The company responded by making preliminary plans to relocate its entire operation to Stowmarket. Fortunately, before the company had committed itself to the move - which was to cost an estimated £500,000 - the Borough Council reconsidered its position and came to the realisation that a factory that employed so much labour should be viewed as a valuable asset.

Not long afterwards the company became part of Imperial Chemical Industries Limited. A further significant acquisition in 1936 was The British Paint and Lacquer Company Limited in Cowley, whose close connections with Morris Motors Limited were to prove of great future benefit. When war broke out in 1939 the company's entire management and office staff moved out of London to join the factory workers at Slough.

Manufacture of Dulux had to be halted between 1939 and 1948, and twice the factory sustained bomb damage. However, the company played a leading role in organising essential supplies of scrim paints, camouflage paints and the special finishes needed for tanks and shells. It was also a member of the Aircraft Finishes Group, a group of seven approved firms responsible for meeting the demand for specialised finishes for aircraft. In addition, incidental discoveries that had arisen out of the extensive research carried out at Slough before the war suddenly took on a new importance when they were adapted to special wartime applications; so urea-formaldehyde resins, and later melamine-formaldehyde resins, formed the basis of a lacquer for the interior of jerrycans.

In 1940 Nobel Chemical Finishes had become known as ICI (Paints) Limited. By the end of the war further internal reorganisation had established the Slough factory as part of the Paints Division of Imperial Chemical Industries Limited. The Paints Division controlled a total of six factories in Britain, of which Slough was the largest.

Production of Dulux resumed in 1948. Within four years

Top: *The Slough site in the 1950s.* **Left, both pictures:** *1950s advertising for Dulux Hi-Gloss and Du Pont Dulux Yacht White paint.*

Dulux had become the leading brand of paint in the professional field. One factor which contributed to this success was that proof of Dulux's durability was now available - it was noticeable that schools and other public buildings which had been painted with Dulux before the war had survived the years of neglect better than the rest. Also at this time the market for 'do-it-yourself' decorating products was beginning to open up, as householders increasingly opted to do their own decorating, rather than pay professional decorators.

At first the company cautiously slanted its early advertising towards the decorating professional with the slogan 'Say Dulux to your decorator.' At the beginning of the DIY movement there were very real fears that it would cause a split within the industry, with the professional craftsmen and the merchants who supplied them refusing to have anything to do with the products which the retailers supplied to the amateurs.

The Paint Division's decision to risk alienating the professionals by putting Dulux on the retail market in 1953 was a brave one. The company had never before sold its products to the public in such a big way, and so had no real experience of promoting its products.

Although Dulux was by now well-known within the trade, the general public would have no reason to buy it unless its advantages were brought to their attention through advertising. So the company advertised. It placed black and white pictures and announcements in the press, it put display material up in shops, and it produced colour cards and leaflets for people to take home.

The company soon progressed to full-page colour advertisements in magazines, posters on buses and railway stations, and other more sophisticated sales aids. In 1955 it was responsible for some of the first

Top left: *A 1950s ICI Paints truck carrying the slogan 'Say Dulux to your decorator'.* **Above:** *An ICI Dulux Gloss Finish brochure from 1957.* **Below:** *A battery of paint mixers in the 1950s.*

SLOUGH, MAIDENHEAD & WINDSOR MEMORIES

going on to account for a substantial market share of both gloss and emulsion and giving ICI Paints Division some 40 per cent of the entire paints retail market in Britain and about 20 per cent of the trade market.

ever television advertisements for paint. And in 1961 ICI's place in the history of advertising was assured when Dash, the first of several Dulux Dogs, made his appearance and instantly won the hearts of the British public.

Digby, Duke, Tanya, Pickle, Dillon, Boots, Holly, Sebastian and Thomas all followed Dash into the Dulux Hall of Fame and into the public's affection. So much so that many people now simply call an Old English Sheepdog a 'Dulux Dog'.

Research had meanwhile continued. A range of emulsions was developed to replace the pre-war 'distemper'. After a great deal of experimentation this product was based on polyvinyl acetate, rather than an alkyd emulsion. Marketed as Du-Lite (later Dulite), emulsion was produced in a range of colours which corresponded to the Dulux gloss range; in the early 1960s the two brands were merged, with both gloss and emulsion being sold under the name Dulux. Brilliant white paint, introduced in the mid-1960s, was a notable success,

By the early 1970s the DIY and trade businesses were split so that the company could meet the differing needs of the two markets. Competition began to grow more aggressive during the decade, but ICI retained its lead; with the market place for brilliant white becoming an area which was contested particularly fiercely, ICI launched its range of off-whites with a 'hint of colour'. The competition followed suit, but Dulux retained three-quarters of the market. Dulux has been responsible for a series of new products which competitors merely copy. The trade and DIY markets have Dulux to thank for such innovations as Duette, Sonata, Solid Emulsion, Decorator Select, Colour Dimensions tinting, Natural Whites, Heritage, Eggshell (based on low odour solvents), Kitchens and Bathrooms paint, Satinwood, and the Language of Colour concept which helped customers create co-ordinating colour schemes.

Top left: *ICI Du-Lite produced in the early 1960s.* **Above:** *1980s advertising.* **Below:** *ICI Paints Headquaters in 1999.*

The acquisition of Williams Plc in 1998 added brands including Hammerite, Cuprinol, Polyfilla, and Polycell to the product range, taking ICI into the woodcare, metalcare, adhesive and filler markets. It also developed a range of coatings for food and drink cans and refinish paints for repairing vehicle paintwork. Its packaging coatings business remains a world leader in the specialised market for internal and external coatings for food and beverage cans and other metal containers, and also includes packaging inks and laminating adhesives and coatings for flexible packaging.

Slough was also a pioneer of paint recycling. In 1995, as part of its commitment to the environment, the company began sponsoring Community RePaint schemes. This involved collecting unused paint from the public, and re-distributing it amongst 'not for profit' groups. Part-used cans of paint suitable for domestic application are collected from specified collection points, and are given to charities, community groups and voluntary organisations. The paint is then used in local communities on projects which would not have otherwise have been financially viable, such as brightening up youth clubs, village halls and elderly people's homes. These schemes are run by local environmental and recycling agencies with the support of their Local Authorities, and provide a very positive solution to the problem of disposal of waste paint; the community benefits, and at the same time landfill sites and refuse collectors are freed from the difficult and messy task of disposal.

During 2008 the Community RePaint Scheme re-distributed 200,000 litres of paint which went to 11,000 beneficiaries all across the United Kingdom and Northern Ireland.

The company's commitment to the environment is just one aspect of its role in the community. Many charities have benefited from both the fundraising

*Top: A range of products produced by ICI Paints/AkzoNobel. **Left and above**: Two examples of the Community RePaint scheme started by the company in 1995 as part of its commitment to the environment.*

SLOUGH, MAIDENHEAD & WINDSOR MEMORIES

performance coatings than those of any other manufacturer. It also makes a huge range of specialty chemicals that find their way into hundreds of everyday products.

AkzoNobel is the largest paints and coatings company in the world. As a major producer of specialty chemicals it supplies industries worldwide. The company's 60,000 employees—based in more than 80 countries—are committed to excellence and delivering Tomorrow's Answers Today.

And none are more committed than those based in Slough.

activities of staff, and corporate sponsorship of events such as the Slough Canal Festival. The company also takes an active educational role. Its series of informative and attractive publications for use in schools provides an introduction to various aspects of paint technology. Educational involvement also includes the annual Dulux Young Scientists competition designed to encourage an awareness of science, technology and innovation in the school classroom.

In the last decade there have been big changes and improvements to the Slough site. During 2008 alone the manufacturing plant benefited from a £3.5 million investment to improve productivity and upgrade site infrastructure.

Meanwhile innovation has never stopped: in 2005 Dulux Light & Space technology offered paint which reflects twice as much light as ordinary paint, making it ideal for brightening darker rooms.

In 2008 the company launched Dulux PaintPod, combining specially formulated emulsion designed for use with PaintPod application technology which allows just the right amount of paint to be applied to a paint roller via a pump mechanism. The Dulux PaintPod also cleans itself.

With annual sales of over 14 billion Euros AkzoNobel's products can be found everywhere, from the Beijing Olympic arenas and Sydney Harbour Bridge to Blackpool Tower and the Cutty Sark – not to mention your own home. More people choose AkzoNobel decorative paints and

Top left: *The Dulux PaintPod.* **Above:** *The Dulux Dog at the Slough Canal Festival sponsored by ICI Paints/AkzoNobel.* **Below:** *AkzoNobel's new corporate brand. Symbolizing the company's fundamental transformation and determination to lead change, it embodies AkzoNobel's clear ambitions for the future and a passionate commitment to deliver Tomorrow's Answers Today.*

Ragus - Specialists in Sugars since 1928

Sugar is an indispensable part of our lives. Our ancient ancestors craved sweetness but for them the only source was honey. Sugar cane has its origins in Asia, and it was in India that sugar in its crystalline form was first produced around 350 AD.

In Britain, however, sugar remained a rare luxury until first the Portuguese, and later the British themselves, established sugar plantations in the New World.

Fortunes were made by sugar planters, but by the Victorian era sugar was no longer a rare luxury but a common accompaniment not only to tea but in cakes and confectioneries of all kinds.

But if the growing of sugar cane was well understood the same could not be said of sugar itself. There are many sugars, and only in the latter half of the 19th century was the mysterious chemistry of them fully investigated.

Not many folk know that Golden Syrup was formulated by chemist Charles Eastick in 1883. Today Charles' descendants still run the family firm he founded in the 1920s. Ragus Sugars is today one of Slough's most important businesses with a national and international reputation for excellence and innovation, the Eastick family having registered more than 11 sugar refining patents since 1880.

In 1882 Charles Eastick and his brother ,John Joseph Eastick, were both employed as the first chemists by Abram Lyle & Sons Ltd, one of around 150 sugar refiners in Britain at the time.

*Top: Founder, Charles Eastick. **Below:** An early laboratory.*

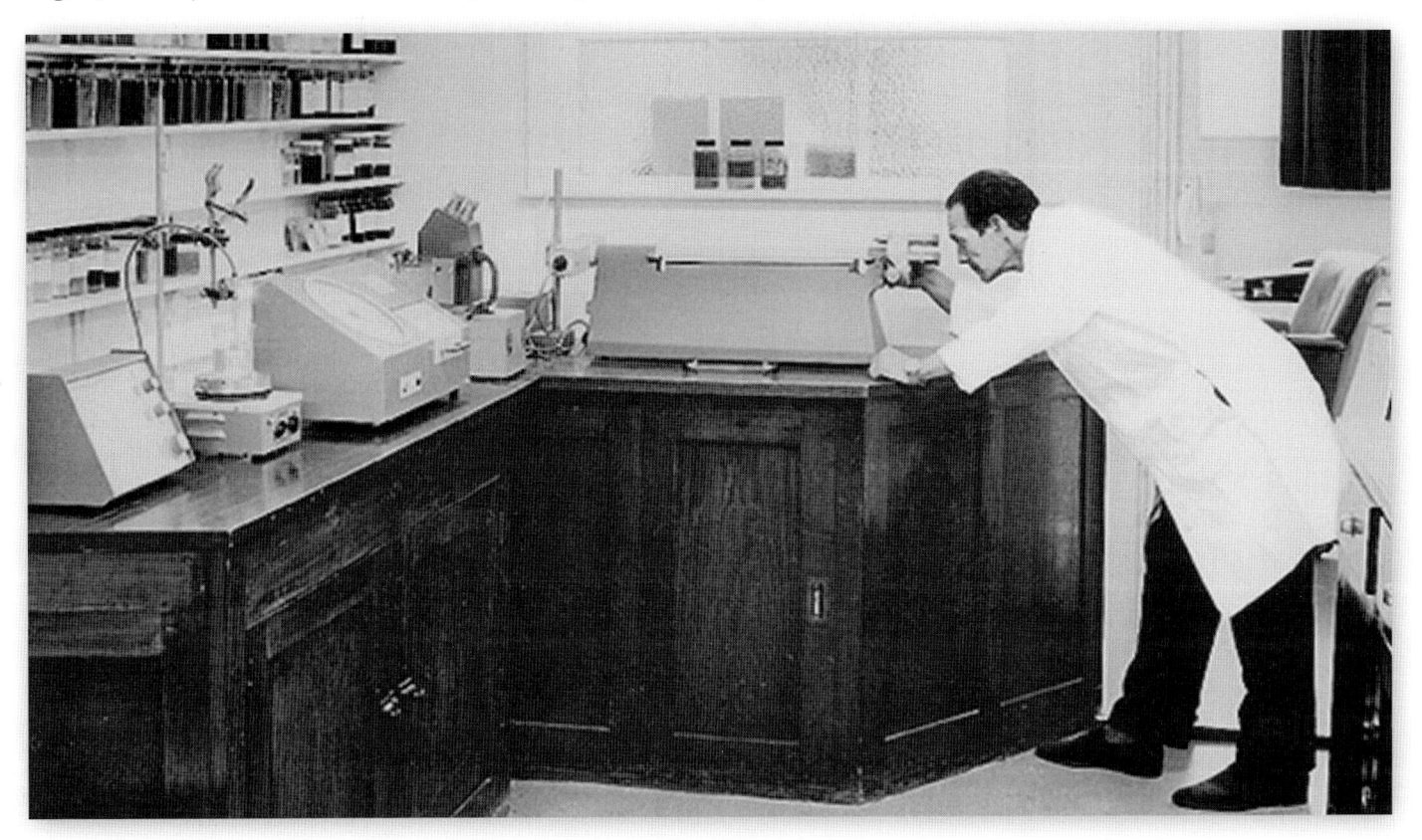

SLOUGH, MAIDENHEAD & WINDSOR MEMORIES

Abram Lyle, a Scottish businessman, had sent his five sons from Greenock to London in 1881 to build a sugar refinery at Plaistow, which started melting sugar in 1883. When problems with cargoes almost brought their work to an abrupt halt, Lyle insisted they carry on working on something else.

The sugar cane refining process produced a treacle-like syrup that usually went to waste - but gifted chemist Charles Eastick discovered how it could be refined to make a delicious preserve and sweetener for cooking. Golden Syrup was the result, made at the start in small but increasing quantities. The syrup was poured into wooden casks and sold to employees and local customers. However, word spread even faster than the syrup - and in a few short months a tonne a week was being sold.

The two Eastick brothers left Lyle's in 1890. John went to oversee the Bundaberg sugar plantations in Australia and Charles to run production at Martineau's Sugar Refinery, at Whitechapel, London - thereby establishing something of a family tradition as his eldest son Fredrick, and eldest grandson, Bernard, also pursued successful careers at Martineau's, with Fredrick becoming Managing Director and Bernard Production Director.

During the Great War Charles assumed a national role, being responsible for administering the UK wartime sugar rationing quotas, for which he was later awarded an MBE.

As the United Kingdom recovered from the first world war, only small quantities of specialised sugars were available, but Charles saw the opportunity to set up a different kind of sugar company.

During the 1920s only small amounts of specialised sugars were being imported to Britain as it was not economic for the larger refineries to manufacture these. In 1928 Charles established a specialist factory on the then new Slough

Top: The Fruit Products Ltd premises in the 1920s. ***Above left:*** *During the First World War Charles Eastick became responsible for changing the industry's emphasis from beet sugar - of which Austria and Germany were major suppliers - to cane sugar.* ***Right:*** *A Matineaus Golden Syrup tin from the 1950s.*

SLOUGH, MAIDENHEAD & WINDSOR MEMORIES

Charles Eastick ran Fruit Products Limited alongside his work at the Martineaus Refinery and was joined at Slough by his youngest son Douglas. Here the product range remained virtually unchanged until the Second World War, when shortage of fruit caused the production of fruit drinks to be abandoned. During the war Ragus focused solely on cane sugars and syrups from Commonwealth countries.

Top, left and bottom: *Past Martineaus and Ragus delivery tankers.*
Right: *The 'Golden Shower' brand of fruit cordials.*

Industrial Estate to produce those sugars, using raw materials from Martineau's, as well as producing cut candied peel and fruit drink cordials made from oranges and lemons. The company - Fruit Products Limited, with the brand 'Golden Shower' – is the longest established company on the estate, having been situated there from the very outset, on the site which it still occupies today - 19? Bedford Avenue.

A sister company Ragus was formed in 1930 to produce 'invert' sugars, mainly for bakers and confectioners. Two years later the companies merged to form Ragus Sugars. The word 'invert' refers to the way such sugar syrups rotate or invert light passed through them, in the same way that light is inverted as it passes through honey

During this period the 'Golden Shower' brand of premium fruit cordials was a major innovation. The surplus fruit peel was mixed with liquid sugar to produce Cut Candy Peel.

120

SLOUGH, MAIDENHEAD & WINDSOR MEMORIES

Douglas Eastick joined the RAF for the duration of the war. Charles came out of retirement to run Ragus, ably assisted by Hilda Osbourne, the company secretary.

Shortly after the war honey was severely rationed. Happily, Charles still had time for one last innovation – 'Golden Shower' Crystallised Golden Syrup. This was sold in grocery shops as an alternative to honey, remaining popular until honey once again became available.

As the demand for honey rose, Ragus began to sell a range of honeys to replace its Crystallised Golden Syrup. In the 1960s, the company had its own bee farms and this led, in 1963, to Ragus inventing Crystallised Bee Candy Feed.

As the 1960s and 70s, progressed, Ragus' sales of raw sugar increased, alongside its syrup sales – 'invert', 'golden' and speciality mixes. The company also started selling white refined sugar and as a result the workforce almost doubled.

The post war sugar industry had seen more and more companies merging. By 1957 there were just 21 companies, though the confectioner/food manufacturer still had a wide choice of suppliers. Twenty years later however, with strikes affecting the British sugar industry, just three manufacturers remained.

Meanwhile, succession passed first to Douglas, then to Charles Eastick's youngest grandsons, Ronald, who ran production, and Barrington, who ran sales. Ronald and Barrington had joined the firm in 1953 and 1955 respectively. Since 1990 the company has been run by Charles' youngest great grandsons, Peter, who runs production, and James and Benjamin, who run sales and marketing.

The majority of sugar refiners had been taken over by the amalgamated company of Henry Tate & Abram Lyle.

Top left: In the 1960s, with its own bee farms, Ragus inventing Crystallised Bee Candy Feed. **Below:** Ragus Treacle and Golden Syrup. **Bottom:** Douglas Eastick (left), Barrington Eastick (centre) and Ronald Eastick.

SLOUGH, MAIDENHEAD & WINDSOR MEMORIES

Ragus was the only private company left; it celebrated its Golden Jubilee under the proud slogan: "1928-1978 and still independent!" It still holds this unique position today.

More efficient ways of working have enabled output to increase significantly. Special bespoke products have taken an ever-increasing role in Ragus' continued success. The raw materials and equipment in use at Ragus today are, however, essentially the same as those used in the 1920s. The range of raw materials is somewhat wider today, and includes many forms of glucose syrups, caramelised, Organic & Fairtrade sugars

Top: Since 1990, special bespoke products have taken an ever-increasing role in Ragus' continued success, by offering their customers tailor-made formulations. *Left:* One of todays Ragus tankers. *Above:* A view inside the Ragus refinery.

SLOUGH, MAIDENHEAD & WINDSOR MEMORIES

and syrups, while more advanced technology is employed in testing of the breakdown of sugars.

To the layman the range of Ragus products is astonishing and surprising: liquid sugars and candy sugars, 'invert' sugar, golden and refiners syrups, molasses and treacles, raw cane, soft brown and muscovado sugars, and, not least, plain white refined sugar.

The main customers for Ragus' range of dry and liquid sugars include the baking and brewing industries, chilled and frozen foods, confectionery, breakfast cereals, sauces, preserves, soft drinks and pharmaceutical manufacturers. In addition to its wide range of standard products the company also produces a wide range of specialist products made to exact specifications and packed either in standard packaging or to customers' own specification.

With a production facility designed to work to short lead times, Ragus has a well-earned reputation for being very responsive to customers' needs. It also has a reputation for being a friendly place to work, with many long-serving employees who have worked with successive generations of the founder's family whose own fathers and sons worked there too.

After more than three-quarters of a century in business, and now the only privately owned refiner in the industry, Ragus continues to be fiercely independent. The company maintains its founder's vision of providing an independent, specialist alternative within the sugar marketplace.

Today there are few firms which have achieved such success without sacrificing their independence, and few families that have such an unbroken history and dedication to a single product.

And that name 'Ragus'? It's just 'Sugar' spelled backwards or 'inverted'!

Top left: Inside the factory. Top right: Frank O'Kelly with staff in the customer service department. Ragus' commitment to customer service has helped build a worldwide customer base, ranging from small companies to multinationals. Centre: Eastick's Golden Syrup. Below, left to right: Ben Eastick, Peter Eastick and James Eastick.

WN Thomas & Sons - Helping the Environment

Now more than ever re-cycling is the order of the day. In Britain alone metal recycling has become a £4.5 billion a year industry. And few firms know more about re-cycling scrap metal than WN Thomas & Sons Ltd based in Stoke Gardens, in Slough.

William Thomas established his waste recovery business in 1850. Since then, this family firm has been dealing with the collection and recycling of waste materials.

Today the volume of regulations coming from the Environment Agency and the EU regulators in Brussels have to be taken seriously. Particularly since 1990, the whole of industry has been swamped with masses of regulations and new working practices not merely to protect the environment but also to encourage recycling of precious resources.

WN Thomas and Sons Ltd was early to recognise its responsibility, both to its own future and in its duty to the environment. In the early 1990s sleeves were rolled up and the challenge taken head on. By 1993 it had the first scrapyard in south east England to become fully licensed - an achievement in which it takes great pride.

To help deal more fully with the safe and efficient disposal needs of today's engineering and manufacturing firms, a

Top: *The winning turnout from the Royal Counties Agricultural Society Show in 1899.* **Left:** *J R Thomas.* **Below:** *A works outing, 1910.*

SLOUGH, MAIDENHEAD & WINDSOR MEMORIES

This would have been an awesome task for anyone, not least for Pat who was only 20 years old at the time.

Yet cometh the hour cometh the man. Pat took over the business begun by his great grandfather with relish. Once it had been a man with a barrow, touring the highways and byways around Wokingham. It had moved through the horse and cart era to a time when lorries first clanked along the roads to Slough. By 1970, this was a business with a turnover running into seven figures. There was a large fleet of lorries, cranes, forklift trucks, a weighbridge, balers, power shears and every other piece of machinery imaginable. Offices had been opened in Stoke Gardens and the future was assured.

Over the following decades the client base continued to grow. People knew that a first class friendly service was guaranteed. The skip collection service has been expanded and there is a balance in the business between the needs of industry and the householder. Even though the company now deals with many large corporations, the 'little man' has not been forgotten. Nickel, chrome, tungsten, steel and more keep the Thomas yards busy.

Today recycling scrap metal is more vital than ever in protecting the environment and safeguarding raw materials for Britain's economic future. And WN Thomas and Son Ltd has both the experience and expertise to help everyone do their bit.

Top left: *A new fleet of lorries arrive in 1958.* ***Above left:*** *At work on the metal shearing machine in 1960.* ***Below:*** *A bird's eye view of the WN Thomas premises in Stoke Gardens, Slough.*

waste transfer station was opened on the premises in 1998. All types of waste could now be accepted. The firm's expertise and high standing in its field were recognised the same year by the Thames Valley Business Enterprise Award.

Despite being a limited company, the business has kept the family-feel to it that has served it well for over 150 years. All of the directors are family members and the staff are regarded as part of that extended family.

William Thomas would have approved of the way the business has grown since 1850. He began in a small way in Wokingham, Berkshire. After some 20 years there the business transferred to Windsor. During the First World War, the collection and recycling of metal became more than just a business; it became essential for the nation's very survival. Railings, sheds, pots and pans were all put into 'the melting pot' to help provide more guns, ships and shells for the war effort. Some of the tanks that rolled their way through the Battle of Cambrai in 1917 owed their existence to the scrap metal merchant and patriotic householders. The same appeals would be made again in the 1940s.

After the Great War the business extended its influence by opening another centre in Slough.

But in 1932, tragedy hit the family with the death of William Nosworthy Thomas Jnr. The huge responsibility of running the growing company fell upon his son, JR (Pat) Thomas.

C. F. Lake - A Firm with Vision

Lakes is Slough's best known name in electrical retailing. The firm offers customers a comprehensive range of quality electrical products for the home, from DAB portable radios to custom-installed multi-room Digital Home Cinema systems.

From its head office at Marish Wharf, St. Mary's Road, Langley, C.F. Lake Ltd runs eight retail outlets. Seven of these are Lakes' multi-brand branches in Berkshire and Buckinghamshire, whilst in Staines, Middlesex, the company runs its Panasonic Store, specialising in the huge range of equipment offered by Panasonic.

The business was founded in Slough in 1947 by Ceril Lake and his wife Mary. He had previously worked for Halidays, a radio shop in Chalvey. Ceril opened a small store at 37, Stoke Road, Slough, where he sold, rented and repaired radios – wirelesses as they were then still commonly known - as well as charging accumulators (large rechargeable batteries).

Ceril fell ill in 1959. As a result his nephew Geoff Mingay (an apprentice television and radio engineer who was then working for Belchers-Chalvey) began helping Mary with the deliveries and repairs in the evenings.

When Ceril passed away later that year, Geoff joined Mary permanently.

Television rental was a large part of business for Lakes in the 1960s and 70s, but as the equipment became more reliable and prices fell, together with easier credit, more and more customers decided to buy. Astonishingly colour televisions cost little more today than they did when they first appeared. More recently the first plasma TV sold by Lakes was a 42" Philips costing £12,000 - today a similar product is only £699!

In 1969 the company opened a new store in Bells Hill, Stoke Poges, selling hardware, tools, garden goods and toys as well as TVs and radios. Further dramatic expansion followed: a store in High Wycombe in 1979, Marlow in 1980, Aylesbury in 1980.

In the early 1980s actress Susan George memorably opened the Dynatron Centre in the company's High Wycombe store.

A Maidenhead store opened in 1990, Bracknell in 1994 and Staines in 2003. A lower ground floor concession with Daniels Department store, Windsor, opened in 2007. The most recent store, Lakes Beaconsfield, opened in 2009. With expansion the

Top: *Mr Geoff Mingay, former Managing Director who retired in 2004 after more than 40 years at the helm.* **Left:** *An early view of one of Lakes Ever Ready window displays.* **Below:** *Store Manager, Alan Amos, in the Slough shop in the early 1980s.*

SLOUGH, MAIDENHEAD & WINDSOR MEMORIES

head office was moved from the Stoke Road store into a much larger central warehouse/head office in Langley.

From just two staff at the outset the firm now has 42 employees, over half of whom have been with Lakes for over 10 years.

Alan Amos has worked for the company since 1975, as store manager at Slough, High Wycombe, Slough High Street and Bracknell. He subsequently became Rental Manager and is now IT Manager. Mark Coster, who started with Lakes in 1978, has progressed from sales assistant at the High Wycombe store to store manager at Marlow, Aylesbury and Slough and is now a Director.

Since Geoff Mingay's retirement in 2004 his son, Richard, has been Managing Director. Richard Mingay began working for Lakes in 1982, starting as a delivery driver and installer at High Wycombe, then becoming Manager at Marlow, Hounslow, Chiswick and Slough before moving into the Head Office.

In the six decades the company has been in existence many changes have occurred in the business: the 1964 switch from 405 lines to 625 lines television transmission, the arrival of colour in 1967, remote controls, Teletext, Video recorders, DVDs, flat screen TVs, 4:3 screen to 16:9 widescreen, Nicam Stereo; the arrival of BBC2, then Channel 4 and CH5 followed by Sky, Freeview then Freesat. Today the latest technologies are High Definition Broadcasting and Blu Ray. What next one wonders?

Nor are these changes the only ones. Many once well known names have disappeared. Manufacturers of televisions once stocked by Lakes which are no longer around include Sobel, Murphy, Invicta, Pye, GEC, Dynatron, ITT, Ferguson, Mitsubishi, Nordmende and Luxor. Today's popular brands by contrast include Panasonic, Sony, Samsung and Bose.

Meanwhile, the domestic installations carried out by Lakes are no longer just the simple television setup. Today's technology can require complete home cinema audio visual systems' together with 'multi-room connectivity'.

Despite competition from multiple retailers such as Dixons, Currys and Comet in the 1970s, and more recently internet traders, Lakes' customer care coupled with quality products has ensured that Lakes continues to thrive.

As for the future, Lakes will continue their expansion plans using the same proven philosophy of the last 60 years, outstanding customer service combined with enviable technical product knowledge.

Top left and above: Lakes Maidenhead (top left) and High Wycombe (above) stores. *Below left:* Lakes' Stoke Road, Slough, store in 1980. *Below:* Geoff Mingay (third from right) welcomes the Managing Director (centre) of Panasonic Worldwide and the Managing Director of Panasonic UK (second from right) to Lakes' High Street, Slough, store in 1988.

Baylis House Hotel - A Jewel in Slough's Crown

Baylis House, in Stoke Poges Lane, is one of the architectural jewels in Slough's crown. Set in four acres of landscaped grounds, the stunning Grade I listed building provides unique hotel, conference and banqueting facilities as well as fully serviced offices in its state-of-the-art business centre.

Today Baylis House has become an immensely popular venue for weddings and receptions, Pre-wedding parties and 'Bridal Showers' as well as special events and Christmas parties, anniversaries, birthdays, corporate hospitality and charity events.

Baylis House was built by Dr Gregory Hascard, Dean of Windsor in 1696 and was later bought by Dr Henry Godolphin, Provost of Eton. The house was subsequently owned by the Osborne family until it passed by marriage to the Dukes of Leeds.

What is open to question, however, is whether Sir Christopher Wren or John James of Greenwich designed the house, as is often claimed.

The original structure may not, in fact, have been designed by either architect, but rather constructed under the direct supervision of the owner as was often the practice during this period.

Baylis House was built in the plain Dutch style of architecture which flourished in England after the restoration of King Charles II.

Over the years the building was inevitably changed by additions and refurbishments and, as a result, evolved from a simple family house to a work of architectural importance.

In 1726 Thomas Rowland, the clerk of works to Windsor Castle, added a third storey to the building.

SLOUGH, MAIDENHEAD & WINDSOR MEMORIES

Between 1733 and 1735 John James, of Greenwich, undoubtedly did work on Baylis House at the request of the second owner, Dr. Henry Godolphin, the brother of Sidney Godolphin, who was created Lord High Treasurer in the reign of Queen Anne. It is also believed that John James built the east wing stable block which is now Godolphin Court. Among his many country houses, James also designed Standlynch (now Trafalgar) House, Wiltshire, for Sir Peter Vandeput between 1731 and 1733. James held a number of public offices throughout his career as a member of the architectural establishment, eventually succeeding Sir Christopher Wren as Surveyor to St Paul's Cathedral.

With such a long history, it is inevitable that Baylis House has been home to many eminent people. Philip Stanhope, the fourth Earl of Chesterfield, was one resident and could well have written some of his famous letters to his son during the time he lived in Baylis House.

Lord Chesterfield certainly enjoyed a better reputation than Alexander Wedderburn, one of his successors. A man of unbounded ambition, he had been created first Earl of Loughborough in 1780, was appointed Lord Chancellor in 1793 and made Earl of Rosslyn in 1801. Subsequently leased to a variety of occupants, the last private tenant of Baylis House was Mary, Marchioness of Thomond, the niece of Sir Joshua Reynolds and ward of Sir Edmund Burke.

In 1830 the Butt family turned Baylis House into a Roman Catholic School which for much of its existence was said to be 'always much more than a school, it was a centre from which, for long years, flowed charity and help for the spiritual and corporate needs of the scattered flock of Christ which in that neighbourhood held to the ancient fashion.'

The fortunes of Baylis House slumped considerably after the school was closed in 1907. The tenth Duke of Leeds now sold it, and a subsequent owner converted it into the Food Reform Establishment.

From 1924 until 1936 it became the Baylis House Hotel during which time a swimming pool was constructed. Slough Borough Council bought the house and 16 acres of surrounding land in 1939 to save it from property speculators. The outbreak of the Second World War however, prevented the council from developing its new property.

During the war the building was used to house various official services, and later as a meeting place for local clubs and organisations. In the post-war years, Baylis House was listed as a Grade I building. This not only saved it from possible demolition or other major changes, but also made the building eligible for grants for repairs.

In 1954 the property was leased to the Urwick Management Centre and in 1996 it was subsequently leased to Towry Law investments.

Today Baylis House offers Banqueting and Conference Centre facilities, with offices and residential accommodation, in Godolphin Court.

Facing page and this page: General views of the spectacular Grade I listed Baylis House.

Office Services

Baylis House offers clients fully furnished offices in an exceptional setting. Experienced staff will take the pressure off running 'the office' leaving clients to concentrate on their business.

The business centre allows users to move straight into an office with no start-up costs and begin working immediately in a professional and friendly environment.

Fully furnished Office Suites range from one person to 25-person offices, many with inter-connecting doors and high ceilings. The offices include modern wave desks and high-back chairs. A dedicated security team is on call twenty four hours a day, ensuring access to offices outside normal working hours and at week-ends.

Unlike many other serviced offices where car parking is off-street or simply not available, Baylis House is able to offer free parking to business occupants and their visitors in a large car park leaving everyone with more time to conduct business and less time trying to find parking.

In addition the impressive Club Baylis Restaurant and Bar is also located in the Mansion House so that business users do not have to go far to have lunch or entertain clients.

Conference and Banqueting

An impressive conference and events venue with a stunning interior has the capacity to hold up to 600 people. The flexible design means it can cater for groups as small as ten.

Above pictures: Office services facilities at Baylis house.
Below pictures: The conference, banqueting and corporate event facilities.

SLOUGH, MAIDENHEAD & WINDSOR MEMORIES

Baylis House prides itself on its high standard of service and attention to detail - an essential ingredient for the success of any event. That's why staff make it their business to understand clients' needs and get it right first time. Clients can rely on fully trained, experienced staff to help with all or any aspect of event planning - from a board meeting to an international conference.

Focussing on both corporate and private clients, Baylis House is able to be highly competitive. With beautifully appointed en-suite bedrooms, clients can choose between a day or 24-hour delegate rate. As for catering requirements - Baylis House staff will provide a first class service from lavish banquet to simple buffet or private dining or eating in the superb restaurant with its renowned international cuisine.

The Perfect Venue
Whether celebrating a wedding, an anniversary, a special birthday or even a glittering Charity Ball, everything one might need can be found at Baylis House.

The stunning entrance with its long sweeping drive will captivate guests from the moment they arrive. The impressive frontage and walls of glistening glass along with the superb surroundings provide the perfect setting for any celebration.

A range of packages is available to meet every need. Whether it is a daytime or evening event or both, the Baylis team will provide the all inclusive package to enable clients to come to Baylis House and be a guest at their own event.

Highly experienced and dedicated staff are delighted to help with all aspects of planning from music, menus, flowers and photography to arranging themed events, discos or live bands.

The Boardroom in the magnificent Grade I listed Mansion is licensed to hold Civil Ceremonies, which means Baylis House can even provide a 'one-stop-shop' wedding service, ensuring a perfect 'special day'.

With four centuries of history behind it Baylis House is a remarkable building in its own right.

Whilst many old buildings have sadly fallen into decay down the years, happily Baylis House has not only been preserved and restored but also enhanced by careful improvements wholly sympathetic to its history and original design.

Today Baylis House rightly enjoys both a national and international reputation.

Not just the building, but also the business it is home to, can rightly claim to be amongst the jewels in Slough's crown.

This page: Many brides and grooms have had their dream wedding day at Baylis House.

Queensmere Observatory Shopping Centre
At the Heart of Slough

For more than a hundred years Slough has been a shoppers' paradise. The town's population trebled in size before the end of the nineteenth century. And like other towns throughout Berkshire, indeed across the whole country, Slough underwent a 'shopping revolution' in the late Victorian era. The high street used to be known as the 'golden mile' as a tribute to the number of shops it contained.

Along Slough's high street could be found almost every kind of grocery, clothing, toy or tool in its dozens of shops.

The late 20th century, however, was to bring some dramatic changes to Slough's 'shopping experience' and today it is The Queensmere Observatory Shopping Centre which forms the epicentre of the town's retail activity.

The original Queensmere Centre with a flint and concrete exterior was built in 1970; it was extended in 1986 and 1999 and refurbished in 1996. The scheme comprises 92 retail units in total 38,300 sq m (412,500 sq ft) and benefited from 700 parking spaces as well as 5,830 sq m (62,765 sq ft) of office accommodation.

A second element of today's centre is the Observatory built in two phases in 1989 and 1991. It comprised 43 retail units in 17,000 sq m (183,000 sq ft); a health and fitness club and 840 car parking spaces. Major tenants then included Primark, TK Maxx, Top Shop and Argos.

In 2000, the internal malls and the central atrium were refurbished along with extensive refurbishment of the cinema and Wellington House and recladding of buildings around the Town Square.

SLOUGH, MAIDENHEAD & WINDSOR MEMORIES

Today the Queensmere Observatory Shopping comprises a total of 596,000 sq ft of retail space - 45% of the retail space in Slough town centre - in 124 shops. Queensmere Observatory is anchored by an 80,000 sq ft Debenhams, Marks & Spencer, Primark and TK Maxx and attracts an average of 350,000 visitors each week – that's a total of over 20,500,000 visitors a year.

Yet the Queensmere Observatory shopping centre has more than just shops for its visitors: the centre also has cafés and restaurants, a 10-screen cinema and a health and fitness club.

As a community shopping centre the Queensmere Observatory runs regular competitions, promotions and events maximising community involvement. And there are community links with schools, charities and Shop Mobility.

Queensmere Observatory, now owned by Criterion Capital, boasts more than 1,400 secure car parking spaces, whilst during the day there are 47,000 people within 10 minutes walk of the town centre.

This is on par with Reading, more than two and a half times High Wycombe, more than four times Uxbridge, more than six times Staines and more than eight times Bracknell.

But where do all the visitors come from? Slough and its shops enjoy a superb strategic location: Queensmere Observatory is just a short walk from Slough train station - central London can be reached in only 15 minutes and Heathrow airport in 20 minutes. It is just a few minutes from the M4, with some of the UK's most affluent residential areas within easy reach, whilst Queensmere Observatory itself enjoys a superb central location - at the heart of major and minor bus routes from the wider Slough area.

Slough's shopping experience looks set to repeat the 'Golden Mile' era of the late 19th century today in the 21st.

The total catchment population of 619,000 is growing, and is set to increase by 5% over the next 5 years. For those who are interested in retail business statistics and numbers the prime catchments by population are: White collar workers 65%, Home owners 73%, Family-orientated over 30% in the 25-44 age group. Shoppers' per capita spending is more than 10% above the national average. Figures are from the Javelin Group and the 2001 Census.

Today the Centre's 'Key Retailers' include an 80,000 sq ft Debenhams, Primark, H&M, Footlocker, New Look, HMV and a Virgin Active Health Club – not forgetting that 10 screen Empire cinema. There is also a new 20,000 sq ft Next store.

What would Slough's Victorian shoppers make of it all? They were keen on progress and were proud of their Golden Mile. Today's shoppers can take an equal pride in their modern 21st century shopping centre.

Facing page: Interior and exterior views of Queensmere Observatory Shopping Centre. **Above:** Having fun at the Easter Bunny Parade. **Above left:** The opening day of a new Next store. **Below:** A bird's eye view of Queensmere Observatory Shopping Centre.

East Berkshire College - Learning for Life

Schooldays are said to be the happiest of one's life. Whilst East Berkshire College cannot guarantee to make every day perfect, it can certainly ensure that every day is interesting and rewarding.

Today the College has over 1,200 students and nearly 800 staff.

There are two main centres - at Langley and Windsor, as well as sites at Maidenhead and Slough. A new £10 million campus opened in Windsor in 2006.

Since Langley College combined with Windsor and Maidenhead to become the East Berkshire College in 1992 it has catered for both young and mature students. For some that next step will come via 'A' level courses: 95% of students passed their A Levels in 2007. For others there are qualifications that are geared specifically towards employment: their high pass rate at East Berkshire College matches those for A levels. There are many vocational courses including forensic science, plumbing, business, construction, engineering, caring, health and beauty, leisure, travel and tourism.

The College main building, Langley Hall, became a listed building in 1949. Its fine 19th century front of red and grey brick leads into the main 17th century house, three storeys high, with fluted raised stone keys, parapet and delightful mullions and transoms. During the Second World War RAF personnel had billets there. In the first part of the 20th century, however, the Hall had been used as an orphanage.

Kittie Carson, an actress famous for the song 'Don't put your daughter on the stage, Mrs Worthington', and some of her friends set up the Actors' Orphanage in Croydon in the late 19th century. Its first President was the most famous actor of his day, Sir Henry Irving.

The orphanage moved to Slough in 1915. Between the wars, visitors included Gracie Fields, Evelyn Laye, Fay Compton and many more. In 1934, Noel Coward became the orphanage's President. In 1938, however, the orphanage moved to Surrey.

Many orphans recalled their years at Langley as the happiest of times. Students who now attend East Berkshire College will too surely one day recall these days as amongst the happiest of their lives.

Top left: *Langley Place as it appeared between 1985 and 1910.*
Below: *A present day view of East Berkshire College from Langley Place.*

SLOUGH, MAIDENHEAD & WINDSOR MEMORIES

Retriever Sports - A Bullseye Every Time

Darts has never been more popular. But where do all those darts come from? The answer is Slough's Retriever Sports Ltd. The firm now set the standards in darts manufacturing and has grown into the largest makers of darts and dart accessories in the world.

Retriever Sports began life in 1973 trading as 'Elkadart'. The business became Retriever Sports Ltd in 1978. The firm was founded by husband and wife team, Tom and Kate Pope, who were then already in their forties.

Tom worked as an upholsterer for British Rail based in Acton. At the start he carried on working full time whilst trying to develop the business in his spare time. Kate worked part time in a local factory.

The tiny business made dart flights and barrels for dart sets. These were sold to fellow dart players in the local leagues. Kate had the job of glueing the dart flights on her ironing board. Thin sheets of plastic were sourced to make the flights, and bars of brass and copper tungsten were bought in to produce the dart barrels. Often equipment was purchased second hand at auctions and from companies that had gone in to liquidation.

The firm originally operated from premises in Mill Street, before moving first to Salt Hill Way, Farnham Road and then on to premises in London Road. Property was also rented on the Slough Trading Estate. Tom and Kate eventually bought the present premises in Petersfield Avenue enabling everything to be housed under one roof.

Tom's brother, Sid, became manager in charge of the machine shop. Kate's sister Doris machined leatherette dart wallets, whilst her husband Norman helped with making of the dart flights. Son-in-law Noel was office manager, but unfortunately died at the young age of 45. Tom and Kate's daughter, Jacquie, works in the general office and son-in-law Ian, former office manager, took over as Managing Director in 2006 when Tom died at the age of 77.

The firm now employs up to forty staff. With its commitment to providing a superior product of the highest quality, outstanding service to customers, innovation in continually creating and designing new products, and investing in the latest technology and expert staff, Retriever Sports will no doubt maintain their position as the leading manufacturer of cutting edge dart products for many years to come.

Today, not just in Britain, but all across the globe, that triumphant shout of 'One Hundred and Eighty' echoes all the way back to Slough.

Top left: Founders, Tom and Kate Pope. *Centre:* A selection of products manufactured by Retriever Sports. *Left, above left and above:* Interior and exterior views of Retriever Sports' Petersfield Avenue premises.

ACKNOWLEDGMENTS

The publishers would like to sincerely thank the following individuals and organisations for their help and contribution to this publication

Slough Museum

Maidenhead Library, Local Studies Department

Windsor Library

The Greville collection

Darryl Moody at Swindon Library, Local Studies Department

Press Association Images

*National Monuments Record (NMR), the public archive of English Heritage.
For further information about these images please telephone: 01793 414600
or email: nmrinfo@english-heritage.org.uk*

All reasonable steps were taken by the publishers of this book to trace the copyright holders and obtain permission to use the photographs contained herein. However, due to the passage of time certain individuals were untraceable. Should any interested party subsequently come to light, the publishers can be contacted at the phone number printed at the front of this book and the appropriate arrangements will then be made.